Mockingbird Ministries
100 W. Jefferson St
Charlottesville, VA 22902

www.mbird.com

Cover and book design by Ashley Rose Walton. Cover art by Caspar
David Friedrich, "Winter Landscape," courtesy of Wikimedia.

Published 2020 by Mockingbird Ministries.
Hardcover ISBN: 978-1-7337166-7-3

Mockingbird Ministries ("Mockingbird") is an independent
not-for-profit ministry seeking to connect, comment upon and
explore the Christian faith with and through contemporary
culture. Mockingbird disclaims any affiliation, sponsorship, or
connection with any other entity using the words "Mockingbird"
and "Ministries" alone or in combination.

Peace in the
Last Third of Life:
A Handbook of Hope
for Boomers

+++

PAUL F.M. ZAHL

This book is dedicated to
our three adult sons,
John, David, and Simeon,
servants of God in their generation.

-+-+-+-

Table of Contents

Foreword

7

Introduction

11   'OK Boomer'

Chapter One

19   "The Shadow over Innsmouth"—Unease within the Last
        Third of Life

Chapter Two

45   Digging for the Root of a Peaceful Outcome within a
        Layered, Archaeological Past

Chapter Three

79   The Present, Relational Effects of a Settled Past—On Your
        Children, Your Spouse, and Your Loneliness

Chapter Four

103   Felt Gratitude—It's More than Just Words, It's a
        Welcome Invasion!

Chapter Five

117   "Where I Am Going"

149   **Chapter Six**
        "Making Plans for Nigel"—Envisioning the Terms of Your
        Last Third of Life from a Position of Peace and Hope

161   **Appendix One**
        Dedicated Listening from Mary Zahl

165   **Appendix Two**
        Books and Media to Help Boomers

173   **Appendix Three**
        A Boomer Playlist

Foreword

PARTS OF THIS BOOK could have been written three years ago.

The endorsement of abreactive listening has been in gestation since the early 1970s, when my wife Mary and I were students at St. John's Theological College in Nottingham, England. There we were taught by Anne Long (later Canon Anne Long of Salisbury Cathedral), as well as by Dr. Frank Lake, who, together with David and Joyce Huggett, gave us the solid rudiments of pastoral care, which our own experience later confirmed.

The emphasis on romantic love as most powerfully incarnating the longed-for human connection with another, and the Other, i.e., God, in human interactions universally—that, too, was something I got early, mainly through life-experience.

The emphasis on redemption and transformation through God's One-Way Love has been confirmed in many situations over many years, both personally and in parish experience. This theology of God's Grace and One-Way Love, a theology shared and widely disseminated by Mockingbird Ministries, directed by our son David Zahl, has been in my heart through thick and thin. That theology came to Mary and me through FitzSimons Allison, retired Episcopal Bishop of South Carolina. Multiple analogies of God's One-Way Love have also surfaced in movies and music.

What is new here, however, with all that, is a renewed confidence in the Supernatural Power of God. Permit the capitalization, for it is conscious.

In 2010 I read *On the Road* (1957) by Jack Kerouac for the first time. In that book Kerouac wrote that "the Negro [*sic*] is the spiritual hope of America." This forward to *A Handbook of Hope for Boomers* is a personal tribute to that statement, its accuracy as I have now experienced it.

In 1998 Bishop T. D. Jakes conducted a spiritual crusade in Birmingham, Alabama, that was intended for African-American men. Jakes is a much loved leader in the African-American church; his picture appeared on the cover of 'Time' Magazine the week of September 11th. His crusade was entitled "Manpower". I was dean of the Episcopal cathedral in that city and called Bishop Jakes's office to ask if I could sit on the dais with him. The initial rebuff I received told me that I had made my request in the wrong way. I was not trying to "horn in" or get some public benefit by being seen up close to the great man. No, what I was hoping for was to sit at his feet and learn from him. The Bishop's sermons on television had impressed our whole family, and he was doing something in them that I wanted to do, too.

When I explained, in person, as it turned out, that all I wanted was to be the bishop's student for the week, I ended up being allowed to sit near the preacher. T. D. Jakes's preaching—the event was for five days and five nights—made an enormous, lasting impression.

Later I began to follow Tyler Perry. Perry would bring his Gospel plays to Birmingham and later to Pittsburgh, where I became dean of an Episcopal seminary. We would take members of our church, and later, students from our seminary, to see these plays. We stood out within the audience because of our white skin. Once Tyler Perry, in costume and makeup as his madcap character Madea, singled out our group from the stage in an off-handed comment. I even got to meet Tyler Perry at a book signing at a Barnes & Noble. There, the cat got my tongue, and I couldn't explain myself properly. Tyler Perry graciously signed his book, *Don't Make a Black Woman Take Off Her Earrings* (2006), "To Paul. Be Blessed!" I treasure that book.

In 2009 Mary and I retired from parish ministry and moved to a town in Central Florida. On Sunday, January 21, 2017, I visited, purely out of curiosity, Paula White's church in Apopka, Florida, near where we live. The church is predominantly African-American, and Pastor Paula's preaching style has deep resonance within the African-American Pentecostal tradition. She herself is white.

Her sermon that January Sunday overwhelmed me. It started a chain-reaction in my spirit and, later, in my thinking, of which this book is a consequence.

Not only did I come to regard my previous confidence in God's 'ability' to change situations and bring hope out of defeat as basically lame and overly diffident, but I came to see Paula and her helpers in the church as angelic witnesses to the Supernatural Power of God. And I came to see this power as one of the keys to finding peace in the last third of life.

I wish to mention the prayer warriors of City of Destiny Church, Apopka, including Sonia Troupe, Susan Hassell, Norman Taylor, Harold Fuller, Elder Marguerite, Minister Luz, Pastor Todd, Pastor Doug, Pastor Brad, Pastor Rachel, Usher Enrique and Joniece, Elizabeth and Cornelius, Officer Ralph and Cynthia, Usher Rob Price, as well as many other believing saints there whom I have gotten to know and treasure.

Jack Kerouac's succinct, predictive tribute to African-American spirituality in *On the Road* arrested my attention when I read it in 2010. His words have come to pass in my life.

Oh, and one more thing: On Sunday night, February 16, 2020, Pastor Paula told me, under the inspiration of the Holy Spirit, that I would write one more book. Others had said, almost to 'blow me off,' it felt like, when I was down—or reassure themselves about themselves—"Don't worry, Paul. You have just begun to fight. You've got a lot more to give." Or, "I guarantee you, Paul, you are good for at least two more jobs before you finish up." But Pastor Paula never said that. Paula just said, "You will write one more book."

This is that book.

I wish most warmly and personally to thank Will McDavid for his wise and persevering work in editing the book on behalf of Mockingbird Ministries. This is the second book on which Will and I have worked together, and ... "Second Verse, Same as the First" ("I'm Henry VIII, I Am", Herman's Hermits, 1965). Neither of us thought we would be collaborating during the midst of a worldwide pandemic! But the coronavirus lent urgency to the project, an urgency that 'worked' in connection with its inescapable subject.

On the Mockingbird team, Kendall Gunter has done a superb job proofing the book and putting the finishing touches on. It would not be "present and accounted for" without Kendall. Simeon Zahl also helped edit the book in the final stages. Simeon's wise comments have made it both stronger and more precise, as well as more hopeful and consoling.

David Babikow has encouraged me warmly and for many years now to get things down, whether in print or in podcast form. He also endowed the initial production of the *Handbook*, for which I am extremely grateful.

INTRODUCTION

'OK Boomer'

WELL, I GUESS I'm one of them. A 'Boomer,' I mean. A member of the soon-to-disappear 'Baby Boom' generation, the ones who were born after World War II, were children during the 1950s, and came of age in the big bump of the late 1960s, when everything we had thought or been taught got flipped on its back.

'Boomers,' for better or worse, are often dismissed today in the somewhat contemptuous ironic retort, 'OK Boomer!' The crowding-out people who dismiss us will soon have their wish. I don't mean that bitterly, for it's a fact. We are dying off and dying out.

The other day I was listing my friends from childhood, the companions of my youth and adolescence. In a flash I counted on my fingers and realized that roughly half of these treasured sharers are dead. As an ordained Episcopal minister, I have even been summoned to perform some of their funerals. One of these days it will be my own.

What begins to happen as you consider your own death, and even at the hopeful distance of 15 to 20 years from the fact, is that your emotional interests, your actual felt concerns, shift a little. For many years you were just trying to survive, juggling a host of responsibilities and duties, i.e., the requirement to make a living; the passionate hold on you of your children (if you have them) and their best interests; the desire to be a well-loved (hopefully, physically loved) and also well-loving husband or wife; consuming inner questions and unwelcome gaps related to your own emotional past, which could still surface, especially when you were under stress from the burden of 'doing it all'; and not to mention the interests and avocations that have kept you sane—from sky-diving to Winston Churchill to old movies to sailing to gardening to Paul McCartney and Wings to stamp-collecting. You name it.

In my early 30s I preached a sermon once based on the cover of an issue of *Redbook* magazine. That cover depicted a woman about my age, juggling eight red balls in the air. One ball read *Career*. One read *Husband*. One read *Children*. One read *House*. One read *Fitness*. One read *Diet*. One read *Community*. One read *Me*.

I called my sermon "The Juggler." Our parish at the time was a fairly up-scale community outside New York City. That sermon touched as deep a nerve in my hearers as any I have ever preached. It seemed to speak to, and hopefully for, many women who were in the congregation. There was almost a rush towards the preacher at the end of the service, of stressed but apparently successful people who wanted a copy of the sermon or wanted to talk about it or give it to a friend.

I identified with it myself! Which is a little strange, i.e., unfair, because it was my wife Mary who was doing by far the most juggling in our family.

Later in our ministry, we sought to excavate the roots of people's exhausting need to juggle so much in the interests of a hoped-for equilibrium. The governing narrative of many people's lives we knew at the time was that if only I could do justice to it *all*, somehow keep my competing stresses in some sort of balance, then I could exist in peace, at least some of the time. Peace!

What we found out, and not just in everyone else but in ourselves, was that such a 'peace,' founded on such a 'balance,' never actually came. Rather, there was this never-ending wheel in motion—we were really rats in a cage—which turned impassively, or, more accurately, un-sympathetically, as in the Journey song about the "Wheel in the Sky." I never seemed to find that elusive peace. Or at least not on those terms.

There was therefore an inevitable questing within us and in our ministry towards the *roots* of the juggling-mentality. What was causing us, and just about everyone we knew, to get caught up in the never-ending pursuit of an unattainable equilibrium?

At that point we embraced some of the insights—many of the insights—of psychology. In other words, therapy. Our beloved teacher in England Dr. Frank Lake, long dead now, used to say, "Don't let your archaeology determine your teleology." We came almost breathlessly back to that insight. What, in fact, was this archaeology, this layeredness of one's personal historic past, that seemed to bear so much 'fruit' for un-ease and lack of peace? Was it a demanding father or an intrusively attached mother or a competition of siblings within our "family of origin"? We examined these issues and learned a lot.

It has to be said, though, that now, in the last third of our lives, the engrossing question from that time, the question of 'balance' being sought within the press of stress, feels less pressing. It feels less urgent. Mary and I do not move as fast, or oscillate as rapidly, from one stress to another. Moreover, several of our big stresses from that period have basically 'left the building.' Yes, we are still hoping for and needing a seemingly unattainable mental equilibrium, but hammer-and-tongs seem to over-kill it. We are just desiring some reassurance, something like the old (and usually phony) mantra we used to hear from Job's false comforters, "It's going to be OK." Our lives on their own terms have not yet resulted in a satisfying sense of reassurance.

As a late-ish Boomer—I am 69—the resonance of my 1982 sermon about juggling is now just a memory. I mean, our lives are so different. Our sons are grown men and have families of their own. My career is in retirement, at least officially speaking. My diet is prescribed, due to health problems, by our doctor. 'Fitness' means walking around the track five times (at most) per day. Our involvement in the community is limited to volunteer projects of local beautification and a few failed attempts to resist over-development in "My Little Town" (Paul Simon, 1975). The one "continuing city" (Hebrews 13:14) I have, in terms of actual, meaningful engagement, is my wife. She is still here. She is still "Somebody to Love" (Jefferson Airplane, 1967). And *Me*? Well, that—*Me*—together with her, is all I really am, or seem to be able "to have and to hold."

The spirit of most Eastern religions would probably say that the transition to what this short book is calling "the last third of life" involves a process of dis-attachment from emotionally important entities from your first two thirds of life. I agree with that. In a way, your body's decline forces you to detach from certain things or interests. You can't see very well; and if I misplace my reading glasses one more time, I think I am going to scream. Then there's your hearing aids, which get left at the barber shop every time you have a haircut. Or you forget to take them out when you're taking a shower, and they are destroyed forever. Moreover, the simple passage of time takes your children away from you, and your career, too—whatever *that* was. (My friend Arbus, who had a big job in journalism for many years, now refers to his "so-called career.") And "Who," to quote The Who (1978), "Are You?" That is still a good question.

On the other hand, some people in the last third of their lives don't dis-attach at all. They are as bound up in older age with their children's lives or their original career aspirations or just their search for outside validation as they were in their 30s and 40s. We have known some high-profile successful men who spent the last third of their lives literally waiting for their next honorary degree to be awarded them from a major university. And a few of them succeeded at that. I would call this attitude a form of anachronistic living. These hypnotized people are not in due season. Eventually, though, illness and death wrenches one's fingers of close attachment away from every visible object. Sometimes, this does not happen until the moment of death. It is not a pleasant way to die.

I do observe that the interests I have in the last third of my life have changed. I didn't try to *get* them to change, nor attempt to procure a more serene life-style or even demeanor. I adopted few 'practices' to slow me down and provide the acquiescence that is supposed to come with 'maturity.' (I did adopt some practices later, yes, but my interest in them came naturally rather than by solicitous recommendation from the outside.) It is just that *things have changed.*

Interest in the maintenance side of life, of almost any kind, has declined precipitously.

By "maintenance," I mean keeping everything going—passports

and Internet PIN numbers and laundry and house-cleaning and the DMV and clothing and car maintenance and details—punctually and in order. We still do those things, but they mostly feel like "chaff which the wind blows away" (Psalm 1:4). Interest in personal publicity and self-promotion, while not dead, has faded. (I know this just because I feel it.) Interest in staying in touch with a million people from our past has, with exceptions, run out of gas. Interest in staying abreast of most things going on in the world has, also with exceptions, run out of gas. (The coronavirus is an exception!) The desire to travel—well, it's either been more or less satisfied, or it feels like work. Airports!

Some hobbies still have meaning, yes. But the hobbies to which one remains loyal seem to derive their strength from the point in your life when they took hold. In other words, if you liked horror movies when you were 10, you are still probably delighted by *The Bride of Frankenstein* (1935). And if you danced to the Four Tops when you were 18, you probably still know the words to "Bernadette" (1967). But if you got interested in Winston Churchill when you were 50, you are probably well on the way to forgetting about "Clemmie," and Blenheim. There are exceptions to these observations, but the downward trend is sure.

The last third of life witnesses a felt decline in the quality and number of the things that mattered to you when you were in your second third. Ironically, the emotional and derivatively intellectual interests of your *first* third of life probably mean as much to you now as they did then, though in the softer light of age and recollection, and loss. But the things that stressed you—and caused divorce, disruption, and dismay—in your second third of life, those things are fading. "Pictures of Matchstick Men" (The Status Quo, 1968).

What things about your life do not fade? What features of the way it has gone are still sharp?

The pain of early loss does not fade.

The pain of early rejection does not fade.

The pain of early (and to the child, inexplicable) disruption does not fade.

Those things, those sufferings, stay with you. In fact, they are almost more powerful now than when they actually happened.

An old friend of mine never tires of saying, when I remind him of a Calvary we shared in college, "That was a very long time ago." He means, what happened then doesn't matter much now, since so much time has elapsed since the original hurt. I disagree.

I believe it matters almost to the extent that it *is* past.

You might be surprised at how many people, when they reach the point or border of their physical death, return to sorrows—and some to their joys—that go back 60 or 70 years.

Not long ago, I was with a man who was at the precise point of physical death. He was a lifelong atheist, an emphatic and disagreeable man who had rejected the Church of his childhood in clear, defiant terms. But at the exact point of death, his lips moved clearly and audibly with the words, "Holy Mary, Mother of God, pray for us sinners, now and at the hour of our death." We were all completely stunned. He was 5 years old again.

Do you remember seeing the classic Ingmar Bergman movie *Wild Strawberries* (1957)? The elderly professor, on an 'accidental' road trip down memory lane to get to the city where he is to receive an honorary degree, passes inwardly through every single disjunction of his long personal history. But when he gets truly to the end of the road—the viewer is to understand that he is dying at that exact moment—all he sees is the ravishing vision of a scene from his early childhood—of his parents, his siblings, and their contentment. That, at the age of 85, is all he sees at the point of death.

The purpose of this book is to try to describe the last third of most people's human lives as accurately as possible, being especially true to the *emotional* vantage point of middle and old age. The inward and actually driving concerns of this later period, which have certainly caught up with the author, cannot be denied. They require a response. They cry out for an answer, as "deep calls to deep" (Psalm 42:7).

The outcome of many persons' lives turns out to be not pleasant. I am often with middle-aged acquaintances who are looking after their parents in extreme old age. It is rarely a pretty picture. Severe physical symptoms, coupled with wrenching, awkwardly expressed emotional unhappiness, makes their parents' departure memorable but only as an unsettling memory, and sometimes even a shocking memory. People will say afterwards, "I prefer to remember my mother before she got really sick. I try to forget that part."

There are exceptions, however. I hope that you, dear Boomer, will be one of them. It is possible to get to the end of your life, its outcome and its great transition, in hope and peace.

That is why this book is entitled *Peace in the Last Third of Life.* I hope that reading it will help you find some.

The plan of the book moves from diagnosis of Boomer discontents to the hope of release from them in the interest of better life-endings with children, husbands and wives, and one's own past. There is a chapter on the 'mechanics' of gratitude. Then the interest shifts to the question of life after death—its possibility and even its shape. The concluding chapter describes what peace looks like 'in practice', or rather, in actual experience, during the final fragile third of one's life.

A Note Concerning Popular Music

Sometimes people ask me, what gave you the idea to do *that* particular podcast? Or to look at *this* particular subject? I wish I could say it was my deep study of St. Paul, or even of Dostoyevsky. But the real answer is usually more like The Dave Clark 5 or the 1970s Sound of Philadelphia (T.S.O.P.). What happens in my creative process—I realize the wording sounds pretentious—is that I hear a song, and something about the lyric or feel of the song connects with me personally.

Take Joe Simon's "Drowning in the Sea of Love" (1972). I heard it the other day while scanning an iTunes collection of 1970s Philadelphia soul music produced by Kenny Gamble and Leon Huff. The extreme, going-down-for-the-third-time imagery of the song struck me as absolutely basic to the tragedy of repulsed love. It is not that I identified with it exactly, but it stirred me, maybe moved me. Within about 24 hours the idea for a new episode of "PZ's Podcast" came through. For me, that is how inspiration, or you could call it just new material, descends.

The reader will therefore note quite a few references in this book to popular music, mostly rock 'n' roll, a lot of soul music, and a general mix of associations, mostly from "My Generation" (The Who, 1965). This can bemuse some readers and, at times, turn others off. But it is the essence of the writer's voice and persona.

In the Fall of 1992 I was assigned my first *Vortrag*, i.e., short lecture followed by discussion, in Juergen Moltmann's graduate seminar at the University of Tuebingen. The subject of the *Vortrag* was the New Testament theologian Ernst Kaesemann's understanding of "powers and principalities" in St. Paul (Ephesians 6:12). I began the talk with a recording of Bob Dylan's 1979 song, "Gotta Serve Somebody." After just two verses on the record player, Herr Moltmann became visibly anxious—as in, "What have I done by accepting this strange American student into my program?" But I kept the record on and was able to persevere through the key verse. Then began the formal paper. Everything went quite well. Afterwards, Herr Moltmann's graduate assistant, who was rigorous, said the song worked.

Try to tolerate this mark of style, dear Reader, if it feels a little 'broad' or unfamiliar at first. Maybe you will come to like it. In my opinion, it opens up areas of subjective response that only music can. In any event, "I Can't Help Myself" (The Four Tops, 1965). And "I Love Music" (The O'Jays, 1975). +++

CHAPTER ONE

"The Shadow over Innsmouth"[1] — Unease within the Last Third of Life

I n 1966 the 'British Invasion' rock 'n' roll group the Animals released their version of "Going Down Slow," a Blues standard by Jimmy Oden. I was only 15 at the time, but the plaintive, grinding, inexorable feel of the song got right to me. Because I was impressionable, especially to music, in those teenage years, the song has never left me.

Recently I listened to the lyrics again, with their driftwood despondency:

> I have had my fun if I never get well no more,
> I have had my fun if I never get well no more.
> All of my health is failing,
> Lord, I'm going down slow.
> Please write my mother and tell her the shape I'm in.

1 The reference is to a 1931 short story by H. P. Lovecraft that is set in a New England fishing village. The entire population of the village is contaminated by the genes of a malevolent race of undersea fish-creatures called "The Deep Ones." The genetic "shadow" over Innsmouth, like the sword of mortality hanging over us all, is inherent, intrinsic, and triumphant. Lovecraft was a nihilist and had, by his own admission, no hope of any positive good beyond the grave.

> Please write my mother and tell her the shape I'm in.
> Tell her to pray for me,
> Forgive me for my sin.
> On the next train south, look for my clothes back home.
> On the next train south, look for my clothes back home.
> 'Cause all of my health is failing,
> Lord, I'm going down slow.

When you are young, you are not programmed to receive such a message. Far from it. You are more like St. Peter, to whom Christ said by the Sea of Galilee: "Truly, truly, I say to you, when you were young, you girded yourself and walked where you would; but when you are old, you will stretch out your hands, and another will gird you and carry you where you do not wish to go" (John 21:18).

It is not as if I am saying we should bark strong warnings to younger people about the 'muscle shoals' of the future, the scuttled dreams and disenchanted ideals of youth and prime of life. Well, actually, we probably *should!* Our story needs to be heard. Our cautions could make a difference to them. But we never *will* be heard, so forget about it. The older generation never will be "heard" by the younger, even if our apprehensions are potentially useful. We will never be heard, that is, until it is very late in the game for our potential hearers.

This is why only Boomers are likely to read this book. (There are lots of Boomers out there, though.)

This first chapter 'on the road' to hope of a lasting peace begins by chronicling the widespread disillusionment that marks the aging process, including the almost universal attrition of health, physical and mental, that accompanies growing old. The focus then becomes the loss of emotional connection that afflicts the elderly. That loss of connection creates a bleak field of loneliness and nostalgia within an enormous section of the population.

'Normal' Disillusionment

Experience of life, one's "Works and Days" (Hesiod, c. 700 B.C.), tends to bring with it disillusionment. And the more life-experience you have, the more disillusionment you get.

This is not true of everyone, for there exist people who are, for any number of reasons, optimistic and hopeful by nature. Such in-born or in-bred optimism is a great gift and resource. It can turn dark attacks of "outrageous fortune" into opportunities and oddly lucky 'chances.'

But there is a disillusionment of experience that is based on actual observation of how the world 'works,' and "so it goes and so it goes and so it goes and so it goes" (Billy Joel, 1989). This is the 'normal' or objective disillusionment that is the effect of empirical observation.

For example, my wife has worked for several years on various projects to beautify our small town. She advocates for the old oaks that line the older streets and she plants new ones wherever they can provide needed shade for the many new houses being built. She works closely with City Hall to coordinate landscaping on the main 'arteries' of our little downtown. She occasionally gives formal testimony, polite but well informed, at meetings of the City Commissioners to determine aesthetic requirements for the new housing developments that are going up all around us at a fast clip.

Yet one day, driving down an avenue just two blocks from the shaded old main street of our town, she is stunned to see—as we all are—that the power company has just taken down every single living thing—bulldozed every tree, old, young and middling—along a full mile of that avenue. Moreover, Duke Power has put up dozens of towering, gigantic concrete power poles, twice as high and twice as wide as the ones that were there before, without even the thought of burying the lines, let alone factoring in the 'freeway' ugliness of the massive concrete poles. "Eminent Domain," they say. It is clear in a flash that no one who lives here, including the Mayor and the City Manager, has had any buy-in whatsoever, not least my Mary, whose hope and work is to the beautification of our community.

My point is not to get in 'the boxing ring' with this particular local catastrophe, for it effectively and arbitrarily cancels in one blow everything that Mary and her colleagues have been working towards for several years. My point is rather to mark the 'normal' disillusionment that such an incident must bring in its train. The incident of the dwarfing power poles disillusions you, in other words, because it nullifies a ton of work and good will without any regard to your feelings, your personal participation, or your personal history. It renders null and void what we *thought* was the positive, philanthropic work of at least one public-spirited citizen.

I could say something like this in relation to a career in the Church. You feel personally called at a young age to give your life, your whole commitment of dreams and hopes and altruism, the essence of what you conceive to be faith in God and the priority of its intended aid to sufferers and sinners. Then you see, about mid-way through your life's work, that the politics of this world has infiltrated the institution you had desired to strengthen. You begin to observe, in one or another encounter with a senior clergyman or 'wise' layman, that the same *quid pro quo*—to coin a phrase—that governs interactions in the fallen world, governs inter-actions in the Church. You had thought that the Church was holier and purer than that.

A celebrated English preacher named Martyn Lloyd-Jones once wrote, "Every institution tends to produce its opposite."

What a thing to say!

Yet I would now confirm his maxim with every drop of blood I (still) have. The very institution I had thought was the bearer of the Word, the Body of Christ, perhaps even the Bride of Christ—well, it's not.

Whether you wish to take it or leave it, one of the chief cornerstones of the mental attitude of persons in the last third of life is something like this:

"I thought my life was going to turn out *this* way." Or, "I guess I put my eggs in the wrong basket." Or, "But we had hoped that he was the one to redeem Israel" (Luke 24:21). Or, "Your mother and I worked so hard and so faithfully in order that *you*, our child, would have opportunities *we* never had."

You can do everything right and get nothing, not one solitary thing, out of it.

The cornerstone of that "Shadow over Innsmouth" which ravages both confidence and courage, let alone acquiescence and serenity, in the last third of life, is 'normal' disillusionment.

"I've got blisters on my fingers" (The Beatles, 1968)

But there is more to the problem of the last third of life and its 'normal' shift from 'all-in' engagement and participation to increasingly distanced skepticism and even repugnance. There is more to the problem than that.

What also happens in the last third of life is that one's personal attachments are— one by one, like your fingers on a metal pipe that is keeping you from falling into the current a hundred yards below— dislodged, whether you like it or not.

It is not a threat to say what I am about to say. It is empirical fact.

Your hearing gets worse. (Costco hearing aids!)

Your eyesight gets worse. (Walgreen's reading glasses—which you misplace every three days anyway!)

Your physical endurance gets cut in half, or worse. (Those UNIQLO sweat-clothes of yours don't even need laundering anymore because you can barely get up a sweat.)

Your physical potency, if you're a man, becomes chancy. (Blue pills!)

Your hair changes color, if you have any hair left anyway. (Dye, for a male—Heav'n forfend!)

Your skin gets blotches and your muscles get stringy. (Botox, maybe? I dunno.)

I can go on and on. It is not as if you can now choose to live—to exist—as you did in the second half of your life. Your body affords you no choice.

We were at church recently, at the really excellent Episcopal parish near where we live most of the year. I asked my wife, because I honestly didn't know, "What percentage of the women in this service right now dye their hair, would you say?" She answered, "About 80%." That was news to me. Because I know nothing, I would have guessed, maybe 30%. Mary said 80%.

But there's more!

Men lose their careers.

The Rector of the Episcopal parish at Beaufort, South Carolina, once said to me that he spends about half of his time at the local hospitals visiting men who have recently retired to the area but have suffered strokes or heart attacks in their first year there. Something about their 'value,' their sense of self-estimation and usefulness, has 'left the building'; and they almost all became vulnerable, with exceptions, to collapse on the golf course.

Women lose their children.

Of course mothers and fathers *both* lose their children—to adulthood, I mean. But for many women I have known in everyday parish work, it is the loss of their children, in the sense of attachment and regular participation (and being needed) in these women's everyday lives, that cuts deeply into their sense of themselves.

What I am saying here concerning men and women in the last third of their lives is not a 'narrative.' It is not a story being made up. It is empirical observation from many years in parish ministry. Maybe the gender element will change with the next generation, when *they* all retire. All I can write is what I have seen until now.

None of these losses, from the at-first modest and then growing health declensions, to the departure of professional significance and also parental significance, is something that you choose. You don't choose it. It *happens to you.*

A physician who specialized in the mental health of very old people once told Mary and me flatly that roughly 80% of the people he treated who were over the age of 75 were seriously depressed. They have little to live for, he observed, little to go on; so they basically wait—watching *Jeopardy* mostly, in the 'lounge' of their nursing homes—for the axe to fall. The doctor did not say this with any degree of relish or triumph, being younger and quite intentional about his own life. The doctor simply stated it with unmistakeable plainness, and also compassion.

So what remains—in the eroding personal reality of your last third of life? The Bible says, in Revelation 3:2, and Bob Dylan sang, in

1979, "Strengthen the things that remain." I am not yet talking about what I hope I can inspire you to instill in yourself and in others as you walk through your last third of life. I am only talking now about *what remains*, in the un-transformed or not-yet-redeemed-and-peaceful-ly-integrated experience that you have already had. What is left to a person from their past when the body starts to go and the active core attachments of your earlier life dissolve involuntarily?

"Precious memories, how they linger, / How they ever flood my soul" (J. B. F. Wright, 1925)

A cliché concerning Alzheimer's patients—it is a true cliché—is that sufferers from this form of memory-loss evince little to no short-term memory but hold much more surely onto long-term memories.

My own experience in Alzheimer's units has borne this out over the years, and with almost impeccable regularity. I was struck early in my ministry by a patient, an ancient bachelor who had never been married, who, whenever I visited him in his nursing home, would always go back to one event in his adolescence. He was far gone in his senile dementia, but of *one event* he never let go. Paul, for that was his name, told me—about 150 times—that he had lied to his draft board in 1917 when his number came up after the United States entered the First World War. He had thus avoided serving in the Army. But he never forgot what he had done. Paul's conscience was bothering him right up to the year 1988, when I saw him for the last time.

So on the one hand, conversations with Paul were a vinyl record on repeat. But on the other, he was a clear witness to the power of an early bad experience to impress itself upon the soul. I was no longer the minister of that parish when Paul died, but I doubt if he ever exorcized his demon from 1917.

My point is that early memories of pain and conflict are indelible. When other defenses come down, early memories of sorrow and suffering remain. What remains beyond all else, in other words, during the last third of your life is the living impression left by suffering from your distant personal past.

We can put it this way:

The biggest block to peace and hope in the last third of life is unresolved, unhealed experiences of suffering from a person's past, usually the distant past, which seem to hold onto you when all or most other attachments, and buoys even, are gone.

The key, therefore, to peace and hope as the accompaniments, indeed the outcome, of a person's physical life and journey, is the resolution of unhealed, unresolved pain from the distant past. That is a maxim to underline and repeat.

It is also a truism the proof of which can be encountered within the life experience of almost anyone you meet. Something took place that was painful. It may have been misunderstood by the person at the time; it may have been intended, by somebody else, as something to benefit the person; it may have been a rejection so whopping that denial of it, inside the person, was the only possible way to live with it, and 'grin and bear it'; it may have been a primal loss, say of one's mother or father, or both of them, that was covered by a thousand cushions from benign relatives or friends; it may have been a childhood disease that the person couldn't even distinguish at the time from normality, because it seemed wholly normal to them. You can fill in your blanks in a thousand ways.

It may have been an abortion at age 17 that you have completely blocked in your day-to-day mind and life. (But it comes up, and oddly, even more so the older you get.) It may be the brother who died when he was five and you were three. It may be the day it was announced to you that you were moving again and would soon be starting another school—for the twelfth time in six years.

It is neither sentimental nor 'anecdotal' to state that the early pains of life stick. The whole world knows this, or feels it, even if it comes out in oblique ways, as in *Citizen Kane* (1941). In that famous movie no one understands that Charles Foster Kane's successful but enigmatic life is entirely driven by the tragedy of having been forcibly separated from his mother when he was a small boy. Only at the end of the movie, in the very last shot, does the viewer 'get it,' and the mystery clears up.

Because the early pains and losses of your life *stick*, the last third of your life is vulnerable to memories of pain and loss, of conscience and conflict, from the distant past. Often it is *one* memory, not many, to which you return, in spite of yourself, or a single bad experience that had several tributaries and enlisted many 'surrogates' in the second third of your life. More often than not, it is one thing.

Unshakeable Unease

The observed principle here is that the powerful emotions which come to the fore during the last third of life represent a 'pole-vaulting' backward to indelible impressions, more often negative and unresolved than positive and resolved, from the first third of life.

The *second* third of life, which was typically consumed with career, family, and 'getting on,' recedes in importance. In fact, the 'progress' of memory loss, which occurs to some extent in almost everyone, is the steady march backwards, to primary memories, and sometimes just one or two primary memories, from the distant past.

Here is a parable to illustrate this.

In 1961 Rod Serling's television series *The Twilight Zone* broadcast an episode entitled "Static." The episode was written by Charles Beaumont. In "Static" we meet a long-retired man living out his unhappy, lonely days in a boarding house inhabited by people like himself—solo retired individuals who are mostly flaccid and bitter, and who watch television most of the day in the sitting room of the house. All of a sudden, the hero begins to hear radio broadcasts from his youth on an old console radio he has found in the basement of the house and which now sits awkwardly in his untidy bedroom. He lights up! These are programs he recognizes from almost 40 years ago. The pleasure he gets from these programs, which it turns out only he can hear, is overwhelming.

The old programs, which no one else in the rooming house proves able to hear—try as he does to *get* them to hear—force Ed, the hero, towards an involuntary crisis of tortured memory within himself. And what we find out is that he took the *wrong* road several decades ago, and failed to marry the *right* girl—who, it turns out, is still living, though in late middle age herself, right in the same rooming house! (The script explains why.)

The power of this episode of *The Twilight Zone* is that Ed's 'blasts from the past' re-open in him the sluices of love and feeling from his youth, and he is able to reach out to his long-lost and neglected love and to re-unite with her. The climax of "Static" has the man literally turning back into the man he was at 25; and she, to the woman she was then, too. As Rod Serling states in his concluding narration to "Static":

> Around and around she goes, and where she stops nobody knows. All Ed Lindsay knows is that he desperately wanted a second chance and he finally got it, through a strange and wonderful time machine called a radio, in the Twilight Zone.

Incidentally, the title "Static" refers to the fact that everything other than the feelings evoked by the ancient broadcasts is just static. Everything other than Ed's long-paralyzed longing for belovedness—i.e., his meaningless-on-reflection career, his current acquaintances, his whole life's journey from age 25 to 65—amounts to little more than static. The metaphor is superb.

Loss of Belovedness:
The Core Threat to Your Last Third of Life

This book is neither a textbook nor a treatise. No, it is a reflection, a series of observations, in part a memoir, of my own personal experience, mirrored over five decades in the pastoral encounters of ordained ministry, concerning the process of aging. You suddenly discover yourself, as I have, in late middle age; and some new reflections start to force themselves on you. Here are two of them:

One, many things that mattered to you during the second third of life stop mattering. I mean, the outward circumstances, let alone the apparent drives, of your experienced life, drop away in their importance. They just stop meaning very much to you. Even when you read a newspaper or listen to cable television, your attention is now at times arrested by different themes and re-discovered interests. This doesn't happen with everyone, but God help the person to whom it does not happen.

Incidentally, the same dropping-away of previous preoccupations takes place during a pandemic. We saw it all around us, and within us, during the crisis weeks of the coronavirus. I had to make myself watch movies, make myself read a book, and make myself be interested in basically anything other than that name: COVID-19.

There are few things more upsetting than watching a man who is still consumed by the task of shaking apples off the tree of his career in order to gain external endorsement or validation. It is embarrassing. It is often a sign, in your late 60s, that heart disease or a stroke is on the way. The marks of success for which you strove during the second third of your life are no longer relevant. They feel anachronistic.

I submitted an essay not long ago to an East Coast newspaper and also to a well-known magazine. In the essay I listed some of my academic 'credentials' in hopes of enhancing the credibility of the piece to the editors. It turned out they had barely heard of the institutions whose 'honors' I once earned. Moreover, the one editor who knew about them said, "Paul, you are coming across as prideful. Drop all the credentials and degrees!" I felt damned-if-I-did and damned-if-I-didn't. Either way, credentials be damned! This was a new and hard lesson.

There are few things more excruciating, too, than watching a woman who is still consumed with the desire to gain her*self*, her view of who she is, from her grown children. She is almost inevitably disappointed—waiting an eternity, as it were, for that adult son or daughter to call or pay a visit.

To round this out, there are few things more upsetting than watching *anyone* in the last third of their life recapitulating their earlier struggle to draw meaning from an outside, visible source. It can be from a dog—important as a dog can be to a lonely single person. It can be from a former student—as in the case of the bereft retired Latin teacher in Terence Rattigan's play *Separate Tables*, who waits poignantly and forever for the visit from a former pupil who never comes. It can be anyone or anything. It is all ultimately about love, or rather, *being* loved. And the pathos of the last third of life is that somehow the psyche, 'coached' by the body as it loses force and substance, returns to *ancient* hopes, to ancient fulfillment maybe, and above all to the ancient aspiration to be loved that is the universal hunger of a man and a woman.

I believe this "Eternal Return" (Mircea Eliade) is the central dynamic of the last third of life.

Thus the **second** fact at the center of the last third of life, is the thing that remains, whatever it was, out of the wilted attachments that constituted your "Light That Failed" (Rudyard Kipling, 1891).

Something does remain. *What remains is the hunger for belovedness.* It is just as 'alive and kicking' in your 70s as it was in your 20s— or in your tweens, for that matter, or even in the first five minutes of your neonatal self. The endless false starts and disappointing objects on which you placed your instinctive aspiration to be loved failed you. "Time and tide" (Chaucer) took them away. But your intention didn't shift, not one bit. The fundamental question of the last third of life is the question of where your belovedness is going to come from.

Bitter Fruit from a Return that Never Takes Place

James thought, as he always thought, that love between a man and a woman was the one thing that made our appalling world endurable, and that without it it was a hell and a madhouse. Such love was ... the only verity.

(Taylor Caldwell, *Bright Flows the River*)

Something I have tried to say often, especially in "PZ's Podcast" on Mockingbird (pzspodcast.fireside.fm), is that it is not love in a broad or *agape* (i.e., non-erotic) sense that is the strongest enduring pull on human beings; but that it is *romantic* love, in particular, that is almost everyone's most famished hunger. In other words, it is the *third* of C. S. Lewis's "Four Loves," not the fourth one, that shakes its flag over the human pathway through life.

I am not discounting the importance of *agape*, i.e., Christian charity and selfless dedication to another's good. But *agape* in the Christian sense is a fruit or effect of prior belovedness, and it rarely functions in the everyday lives of people as does the overriding drive for erotic connection. *Agape* is initially an abstraction, in other words, which does not exist inherently in human nature, but comes, to quote the title of Edith Wharton's supernatural tale of ultimate consequences, "Afterward." "We love"—in the *agape* sense—"because He first loved us" (I John 4:19). What we are born with naturally is a hunger for connection that is solved in the initial situation only by a physical or erotic tie. *On the ground*, in other words—on the ground of everyday human relationships—*eros* is the observable 'ruler of the roost.' To mix the metaphor, *eros* causes the biggest splash. We see this every day, from the bedroom to the songs that are the soundtrack of our lives to the divorce courts.

There is a revealing paragraph in H. Rider Haggard's book entitled *She and Allan* (1921) that mirrors this observation concerning romantic love. Haggard's mystical literary territory was exactly this: the hold of a desire for romantic connection on a person not just during youth and adolescence, but right up to one's last breath! So emphatic and persuasive was Rider Haggard on this theme that both Sigmund Freud and Carl Jung regarded Haggard's novel *She* (1887) as the most profound book of its era. That is not an overstatement. Both Freud and Jung said it in print, and the first German edition of Rider Haggard's *She* never left Freud's consulting-room desk in Vienna.

At one point in Haggard's later novel *She and Allen* there is a kind of throw-away line that I find unforgettable. The novel's hero, Allan Quatermain, has just come upon the scene of a tribal massacre. One tribe's encampment has been destroyed, and all of its inhabitants either murdered or led into slavery by another tribe.

From under a bush, Allan hears some cries of acute physical

pain. They are coming from an old woman who lies there mortally wounded from a spear wound. This is how Haggard describes the woman's death:

> She said that the Amahagger had attacked the village and killed all who could not escape. ... She had been wounded by a spear and fled away into the place where we found her, where none of them took the trouble to follow her as she "was not worth eating." ...
>
> All of this the old woman told us quite briskly after she had drunk the water we gave her, I think because her wound had mortified and she felt no pain. Her information, however, as is common with the aged, dealt entirely with the far past...
>
> While Robertson and I were wondering what we should do with the poor old creature whom it seemed cruel to leave here to perish, she cleared up the question by suddenly expiring before our eyes. Uttering the name of someone with whom, doubtless, she had been familiar in her youth, three or four times over, she just sank down and seemed to go to sleep and on examination we found that she was dead. So we left her and went on.
>
> (Chapter VIII, "Pursuit")

For me this incident in *She and Allan* is unforgettable. That is because the author puts into spare, laconic words the universal experience of the elderly and the dying, by which the memory and evocation of distant past belovedness is the mantra and the rubric at the end. The woman is remembering either a man she loved or a child she bore, and that is her last thought on earth.

"Philippe!"

Almost exactly the same tale is told, though within a different context, in the novel *Gone with the Wind* (1936) by Margaret Mitchell. In that celebrated story, the heroine's mother, Ellen O'Hara, is the most dutiful, conscientious, and prudent maternal influence in the world. Ellen is the only one capable even in the least degree of restraining her petulant, fierce-willed daughter Scarlett from successive errors deriving from extreme reactivity and passionate anger. Ellen O'Hara is the Wonderful Counselor to her entire family.

At the age of 35, however, Ellen dies of typhoid fever. Something odd takes place when she dies. Ellen O'Hara's last word, repeated twice with extraordinary feeling, is "Philippe!" Ellen's all-knowing nurse and factotum, Mammy, is taken aback by her mistress's dying words and remains mystified by them.

"Philippe" is in fact "Philippe Robillard," the young cousin with whom Ellen at age 15 had fallen in love. Philippe had been sent away because the families considered it an inappropriate match. He died soon afterwards in a bar-room brawl out West. Yet when Ellen died two decades later, notwithstanding the father of her children, her children themselves, and the many others whom she had loved well and faithfully, the name "Philippe" was on her lips.

I think Margaret Mitchell understood a lot about human inwardness.

There is a wonderful line in Rachel Crothers's 1937 play entitled *Susan and God*, which was made into a splendid movie in 1940 starring Joan Crawford and Fredric March. A secondary character named Irene, a shrewd and passionate woman played by Rose Hobart in the Hollywood version, having been 'found out,' in relation to an extra-marital affair, by a religious woman who happens to be an old friend, avers simply this: "Why do people never say what they are really thinking?"

Rachel Crothers, like Margaret Mitchell, got it right. What you see is seldom what you get, especially in terms of suppressed pain and the long-term compensations/adjustments that go along with it. If you don't think this is true, if you think I am being overly pessimistic, ask yourself how transparent you are. When was the last time you told someone the whole truth about yourself, in almost any area of life? I will tell you one thing: that time you did tell somebody the whole truth, your life was never the same again.

Objection

The following objection comes up sometimes when I talk about romantic love as the 'be-all-and-end-all' of human aspirations.

People say, "Well, yes, romantic love's undoubtedly important. But isn't it just *one* category or subset—a very important one, at that—of the great, broader experience of love in general? Aren't you turning youth's romantic horizon into something a little wider than it is?"

Yet I hold to my view when people say that, because Rider Haggard's description has always seemed truer to life. When people start to lose their mental and physical strength and are left primarily with inwardness, they return to the memory of their deepest human connection. And that is often in the context of an early romantic burst, as in the *Twilight Zone* episode "Static." It is one quality of memory that is almost impossible to shake, for the hope of the human soul for connection with another human soul is tied to the eternal part of us.

When you fell in love with that man, it felt like the deepest part of you 'answering' to the deepest part of him. Perhaps it didn't happen just once, but it did happen, on "Some Enchanted Evening" (*South Pacific*, 1949).

Listen to your own thoughts as you age. Listen to your inward reminiscences. Not the reminiscences of other people, just your own (most) private reminiscences. Listen to what you rarely if ever talk about, the hidden compartment/s of the complex layered archaeology of your early pain. There is almost always something there. It tends to come out and re-emerge within consciousness during the last third of life.

Here is how Huey Lewis and the News put it in 1985:

The power of love is a curious thing,
Make one man weep, make another man sing,
Change a hawk to a little white dove,
More than a feeling, that's the power of love.
Tougher than diamonds, rich like cream,
Stronger and harder than a bad girl's dream,
Make a bad one good, make a wrong one right,
The power of love will keep you home at night.
Don't need money, don't take fame,
Don't need no credit card to ride this train.
It's strong and it's sudden and it's cruel sometimes,
But it might just save your life.

"Sideshow" (Blue Magic, 1974)

A powerful expression of the 'backstory,' which is really the 'front-story,' of human connection, its decisive fulfillment and its equally decisive disappointment, is a song released by Blue Magic in the summer of 1974. It became Number One on the Rhythm and Blues charts and Number Eight in the U.S. over all. Here are the lyrics:

Step right up, hurry, hurry, before the show begins, my friends.
Stand in line, get your tickets, I hope you will attend.
It'll only cost you fifty cents to see
What life has done to those like you and me.
See the man with the broken heart, you'll see that he is sad,
He hurts so bad.
See the girl who has lost the only love she ever had.
There's got to be no sadder show to see.
No doubt about it, satisfaction guaranteed.
...
See the man who's been cryin' for a million years,
So many tears.
See the girl who's collected broken hearts for souvenirs.

It's more exciting than a one man band,
The saddest little show in all the land.

I think "Sideshow" by Blue Magic tells the truth. People resist this "saddest little show" when I talk about it. But the best songs about it almost always rise to Number One.

Connection Is Everything

Look, these thoughts about romantic love are pretty universal within the world of popular music and film. And that is not an eccentric source or secondary pool. Please don't look down your nose at "what makes the world go' round." Even Gilbert and Sullivan said it (in *Iolanthe*), for crying out loud, and they weren't being satirical.

It is the men who will verify this best. And the entire history of 'soul music,' by the way, from Otis Redding to Bobby Bland to the Temptations to Gamble & Huff. What the men tell me is, "Paul, you are getting a little too close to home with this. Don't uncover what we are really thinking. Better to keep a lid on it." Better "Keep It Hid," as Jimmy Webb wrote and sang in 1968. Linda Ronstadt, too, exactly 20 years later.

I do note that women my age are able to be more focussed, at least in principle, on their children and grandchildren than on that impossibly opinionated man with whom they had once resolved never to 'do lunch' during the epoch of retirement. What did Dr. Lake suggest that other-directed women say to their men who demand too much:

"Oh, go suck oranges!"

Many men seem to be different from many women on this point. After all, most of those heartbroken 'soul songs' were written by men. They reflect male views, both of female-deification and also of female-objectification. But when a man loses a woman, even if it's his mother, "It's a Rainy Night in Georgia" (Brook Benton, 1970).

The point remains. *Connection is everything.* You lost it with your son and you want it back. You would do anything to have him back. You lost it with the wife of your youth—who is still your wife—and you want it back, and especially in one persisting area. You lost it with 'Daddy's Girl,' and she lost it with her 'Daddy.' And you want it back so much. She does, too.

Can you live without connection? Not happily, even if you have everything else.

Can you die without connection? Only unbearably!

The core issue for Boomers, as for everyone who has ever made it through the second third of their lives to the last third, is the loss, or the imminent potential loss, of belovedness.

"Reelin' in the Years" (Steely Dan, 1973)

Let me ask you a question: Which 'oldies but goodies' do you prefer? What music do you like to listen to these days as you get older? To what songs from the past are you attracted?

I would be surprised if it weren't the popular songs of a specific and sometimes very specific period in your life. People are sometimes unwitting in this area, but their latent emotions *lead* them. Someone will say, "I just love E. L. O. [i.e., Electric Light Orchestra]. Their music does something to me." And I say, "But when did you develop your love of ... E. L. O.?" The honest answer is almost always, "I associate E. L. O. with a period in my youth when I was terribly happy and in love with so-and-so." Or, "I associate E. L. O. with a period in my youth when I was terribly unhappy and feeling quite alone, rejected, and bereft."

Or I ask, "Hey, what about 'Farmer's Daughter' by the Beach Boys? Why do you keep going back to that period of the Beach Boys? I mean, what about 'California Girls' and 'Good Vibrations'? They're better musically than 'Farmer's Daughter,' aren't they?" Then *they* say, "Oh, I don't know. I just like it." LIE! (Not a conscious lie maybe, but an unconscious one.) You like "Farmer's Daughter" because it brings back the echo of a feeling, a life-whooshing feeling of absolute connection and power that you once for five minutes had. You had "fun, fun, fun, 'til your daddy took your T-Bird away."

For myself, when I wish to return to the roots, the emotional and sustaining roots, of my love for Mary, my wife of now almost 47 years, I go back to ... Steely Dan. In particular, I go back to Steely Dan's first big single, "Reelin' in the Years." Why do I do that? Because that song was playing on her car radio almost every night when she would pick me up from my barren room in Cambridge, Massachusetts, after her shift was over at Mass General Hospital; and we would go hurtling down Memorial Drive to the restaurant where we'd have supper. We did have "Fun, Fun, Fun," and her Daddy didn't take her T-Bird away! "Reelin' in the Years" never fails to evoke the first great rush of my romantic feelings towards Mary.

To tell you the truth, I keep a playlist of songs on my iPod that never changes. The playlist is entitled "1973." It simply gives me every single song I can remember from the first half of that year, when I was discovering Mary in Boston. I had known her a little a few years before, but not really. But when the *connection* between us began to form, and in me it formed fast, then every single song which was "in the air tonight" (Phil Collins, 1981) become indelible, instantly! So on my "1973" playlist, which I have until now kept to myself, I don't even list the songs by their titles. It's just "Track 1," "Track 2," "Track 3," and so on. Yet Johnny Winter and Johnny Nash and the late Hollies and the early Allmans and the late Four Tops and the Isley Brothers and the Doobie Brothers and the O'Jays and—well, these songs are garlands around my heart and (please, non-hippy) headbands around my brain.

Moreover, I'm the lucky one—the "Fortunate Son" (Creedence Clearwater Revival, 1969)! For I still have her. She is still alive, and we both are. I still have by my side the woman I love whom I have known for 51 years. And her brightness and her smile and sheen are rooted—anchored—in an overwhelmingly stirring past (to me) that lives in fullest glory when I hear that song. (Or for that matter, "Smoke on the Water," by Deep Purple. So there!)

During that exciting time I also made Mary go with me to see *Night of the Living Dead* when it was still a thing in Boston. Will she ever forgive me?

Gerald Heard at LaVerne

In July 1941 a group of Quaker, main-line Protestant, and incipient 'New Age' thinkers gathered at LaVerne College in southern California to discuss in religious terms the prospect and implications for Americans of a coming World War. The informal convenor of this "LaVerne Conference," as it came to be known, was Gerald Heard. Heard, whose full name was Henry Fitzgerald Heard, was an Englishman of Low-Church Anglican patrimony who sought insight from a variety of spiritual traditions, and especially from Quakerism, first, and later, from Eastern thought.

Something that Gerald Heard said at LaVerne, as recorded by the novelist Christopher Isherwood, who was also present, made a big impression on me as I began, against my will, I have to say, to ponder what it meant to be entering the last third of my life. Heard said, "If you want to find God, go back to where you lost him."

The speaker freely admitted that this wise counsel derived from the medieval Christian mystic Meister Eckhart (1260-1328). But I heard it first from Heard, and Heard for me is an unimpeachable source.

"If you want to find God, go back to where you lost him."

What does that mean? I think it means, first, that you probably lost the authentic voice of your true self almost the moment you started attaching significance to the 'static' of the life around you, i.e., the supposed goals of life you established for yourself and also for those you love. Those goals could be financial security, outward affirmation and credit for yourself and your performance, and control or power (authority) in relation to the outward circumstances, challenges, and obstacles of life as they come at you from almost anywhere at almost any time.

The Classical, i.e., Greco-Roman, way of putting this was that everyone who has the least ambition for themselves seems to want **Power**, **Money**, and **Honor**. I have already said that these perceived 'goods,' i.e., Power, Money, and Honor, are typical of the things for which most people strive, to one extent or another, during the *second* third of life. They absorb our conscious attention from our 20s, and sometimes earlier, through our 60s, and sometimes later.

Yet Power, Money, and Honor inevitably pale during the last third of life. They fade in conscious importance and feel increasingly anachronistic. They are superannuated by physical and mental circumstance.

You lose **Power**, by definition, as cancer or heart disease threatens you, as your bodily control over yourself loses ground, and as you become physically, like it or not, 'a mere shadow of your former self.' You can barely remember the name of one person over whom you used to have 'power', let alone the many who now have power over you!

You lose **Money**, or you are bound to eventually, because the markets fluctuate even in the best of all fortunate worlds. Holding on to money for the duration is very hard to do. COVID-19! Or is it true that 'the rich get richer' – that 'deep pockets' are shielded from loss and fluctuation? That is not my experience. Guess I have just known many individuals who once had money, or access to money; but who find themselves living now in a basement 'guest-room' dependent entirely on one of their adult children's generosity. In my parish experience, at least, something like that has been the rule rather than the exception. Your money can disappear within one bad day.

And you lose **Honor**, because fewer and fewer people are still alive out there that have even *heard* of you. Remember the scene in *Tender Mercies* (1983) when the faded country music singer, played by Robert Duvall, is walking down the street, and a lady stops him and says, "Hey, Mister, weren't you Mac Sledge?" He replies, "Yes, Ma'am, I was."

In sum, you lose, lose, lose.

But you have got to find! You have got to find something. You require something onto which you can lay hold, something solid. If only because you are gradually skidding down an increasingly steep plane, which invariably and inevitably leads to the edge of an abyss into which death throws you no matter what you think you'll find, if anything, on the other side of your radical, invisible fall. Will it be an instantaneous crushing on the rocks below? Will it be the strong hands of angels, holding you up? Will it be a trampoline, bouncing you stunningly up and back? Will it be the opening (and widening) scene of *What Dreams May Come* (1998), in which the just-expired Robin Williams walks through Grand-Canyon "gates of larger life" (Book of Common Prayer, 1979)?

If you die with nothing solid on which to hold, and if everything you used to have you no longer have, then you are, as St. Paul said, "of all men most to be pitied" (I Corinthians 15:19).

Gerald Heard said that if you want to find Solid Ground, go back to where you first got off the paved road. Like Christian in *The Pilgrim's Progress* by John Bunyan, you have kept deviating from the stated way that is right; and every time you have, you have had to *re-trace your steps*. To make serious progress in the inward life, and I believe you could also say in the spiritual life, you have to keep going back. In order to go forward you have to go backward.

This is not what everyone wishes to hear. Or at least, it is not what one usually hears.

Life Coach to Nowhere

Here is what I 'wish' to hear; or rather, what I *do* hear most of the time these days when I am struggling within the last third of my life:

"Look, my friend, you are in a new season. I realize you are coming up against impediments and blockages that feel new. I realize your body isn't giving you the performance you expect of it. I realize, too, that you have done some things, and left undone some other things, that you'd like to have done differently. But hey, it's a new season! Your aging, and even the approach of your 'passing,' are part of 'The Circle of Life.' This is the fourth quarter, it's your last lap! Make it a good one. Try to end well."

I maintain that this is pathetic advice! (By the way, please never, *ever* use the word "season" again to refer to anything other than "winter's passed, spring and fall" ("Nathan Jones," the Supremes, 1971). That goes for "transition," too.) There is no comfort in the words, at least if you are on the receiving end of them. Maxims cannot mend you, and especially when they are not in service of the true state of affairs.

Why is there no comfort in the above? Because hearty imperatives fail to minister to the weeping, heart-breaking memories of loss and regret that lie at the bottom of most psychic misery. There is no recognition, in the above cheers from your 'life coach,' of the bleakness and helplessness of the Heathcliff/Cathy side of life—the Paul Dombey/Floy Dombey side—the you-and-your-long-ago-left-the-family-father side—the "Oh Sherrie" side of your Steve Perry record collection. The advice that deploys "go get 'em" jargon to coach the hell out of your impotence and surprised later-life enervation, papers over the cracks of the problem. There is zero recognition within it of the inescapably tragic element in life, and especially the tragic element in your life.

Most 'coaching' platitudes come out of superficial diagnoses of weighty, grave, and chronic inner struggles. They are mostly proffered in the interests of denial.

Footnote from "the Ice Man"

The other day I was walking—I can no longer jog very comfortably—around the track near our house.

As I was listening through my ear buds to Jerry Butler's 1969 single "Only the Strong Survive," I was catapulted back to the spring of that year, the spring of 1969, and to a dorm room in Chapel Hill, North Carolina. There, in front of the small regulation-size mirror the dorm provided us, my freshman roommate Archie was spiffing up his ROTC uniform on the way to afternoon drill. Archie's entire life was ahead of him. He was about to be named Best Freshman Cadet of the UNC ROTC unit, and he was also about to be voted Outstanding Pledge of our incoming class in a social fraternity we both loved. Archie and I were sharing our lives. We were also sharing the experience of two concurrent undergraduate love affairs. And we would listen with great pleasure to Jerry Butler, who was known at the time as "the Ice Man."

Only a few months later, Archie would be dead, drowned in a freak sailing accident on the Rappahannock River. Only a few months later, I would be broken up with my college girlfriend, a relationship that Archie had blessed from the first day of our freshman year. And only a few months later I would be on my way to a different school, far away, and to an almost unrecognizably different life. "Only the Strong Survive" makes me cry to this day, exactly 51 years later. Just hearing the first bars of our Ice Man's' single is enough to bring Archie back, looking brilliantly ready and open for life in his polished shoes, bright gold tie clip and gleaming white hat with the USN insignia. It is enough to bring *me* back, now sadder, if hopefully a little wiser.

Almost nobody remembers Archie now outside of the annual blooming recipient of the award that still bears his name for Best All-Around Senior at Episcopal High School in Alexandria, Virginia. And I believe a few of his fraternity brothers paid for a brick to be inscribed in Archie's memory at the entrance to the new Delta Upsilon House at Chapel Hill. Just writing this down summons an ocean of tears.

Intimations of Mortality

What this chapter began by calling the "unease within the last third of life" is more than a sense of diminution, though it is that. It is more than a Sword of Damocles, consisting of a general anxiety before the pressing fact of death, though it is that, also.

The unease inherent in the last third of life is a prompt which hangs over your whole outlook and is expressed by the phrase "intimations of mortality" (play on William Wordsworth, 1804). And one's clearest "intimations of mortality" consist not of a vague anxiety concerning a coming "end of the world as we know it" (R. E. M., 1987), but rather a dark field of unresolved, unfelt pain from the *first third of one's life*. That dark field, which is the weight, burden, and stress of memory, is the center and circumference of this first diagnostic chapter, the aim of which, when you see it and feel it, is to heal you in relation to it and deliver you from it. Remember that Wordsworth's complete title for his inspired poem is "Ode on Intimations of Immortality from Recollections of Early Childhood."

In 1983, right about the beginning of the second third of my life, I wrote my first book. It was called *Who Will Deliver Us?* I stand by that book today and its conclusions. But the book you are reading now, entitled *Peace in the Last Third of Life*, is its sequel.

Who will deliver us now?—from stubborn and inhering bad memories, inward unease and regret, unstanchable wounds, and holes—pot holes!—that were never repaired. Those inward scars and disabilities have been there a long time. It is time to get out from under them. Or die trying. They need to lose their defeating and vitiating influence over you. And whether you try to get out from under them or not, you will die in any event. Therefore, the matter is "Urgent, urgent, emergency" (Foreigner, 1981). ┼┼┼

CHAPTER TWO

Digging for the Root of a Peaceful Outcome within a Layered, Archaeological Past

Now run away and play with your toys. I've got some thinking to do.

(Taylor Caldwell, *Bright Flows the River*)

T he purpose of this book is to offer some peace and hope for the last third of your life.

I could talk about exercise and diet. I could talk about community and the importance of having people around you who care about you. I could talk about outside interests and community service and keeping yourself 'outward'-oriented.

I could also talk about alcohol and the perils of a sedentary lifestyle. Or the tendency, especially among older men, to withdraw from the world of people and ... watch television or read all day. I could talk about regression to depression and the clouds of false, one-sided interpretation and angry, embittered attitudes that color the conversation of many as they start to seriously age.

I could talk about several disparate but complementary elements, both of diagnosis and of treatment.

But that would mostly be worldly wisdom and what the Pentecostal Christians I have come to know term "the natural." I would be giving admonitory advice, as it were—others can do a better job at that than I—and expecting, hoping "against hope," that a little of it might rub off on Boomers ... a little.

But that is not the cure offered by this particular handbook.

The cure being offered here is the lifting up and out of un-healed memories and conflicts from the past which are, in my experience both of myself and of pastoral ministry, the bottom line of the aging process. The hope of healing for one's ingrown past pain is the most important resource and promise for the person being slowly eroded by the body and the mind's degeneration. And I haven't even mentioned the Supernatural Power of God.

Cries and Whispers (1972)

Twenty years ago an Episcopal minister lay dying in a hospital outside Ossining, New York. I did not know him well, but I knew him a little. For some reason I still don't understand, he asked to see me. As I entered his room, or rather his bay, for we were in the Intensive Care Unit of a medium-sized suburban hospital, his middle-aged daughter told me that the doctors gave him about 12 hours to live; but that he was insistent about seeing this priest, me, from a neighboring parish. The man was 'High-Church,' and I am 'Low-Church.' The man had always seemed to me to be fussy and somewhat stinting, as a personality, I mean. I did not really like the man, to tell you the truth.

But when I got near him, and put my face right up to his, he quietly told me an astonishing thing about himself, for which he desired the forgiveness of God. He said that he could not die until he had gotten it off his chest. Now I am not a Roman Catholic. But right there and then, after he had said what he said in the firmest sorrow, I pronounced the ancient words of Absolution. (This priest and I did share a love for the 1928 Prayer Book.) Immediately after that, he said, crisply but feelingly, "Thank you," and went back to sleep. He had not been in a coma, but everything was in fits and starts.

I left after hugging the man's daughter who was waiting outside the bay. She didn't ask me what her father had said.

Three hours later, she called me to say that her father had died. She said that he had died peacefully.

How could one go through an experience like that without gaining the impression that dying people, like living people, hold many secrets and many hurts and many regrets? This man, in particular, felt a grave burden of regret for which he needed—required—the mercy of God's Grace. Only then could he die in peace. Those were his words. And I believe he did die in peace.

How could you take people fully at face-value again after something like that?

Or rather, how could you accept the 'front' they put on if you knew a person was capable of carrying a burden as heavy as my priest-brother had been carrying? He had carried it for decades. No wonder the Alfred Hitchcock movie *I Confess* (1953) became a favored resource later in teaching seminarians about the pastoral ministry.

Atomic Explosion

After several encounters over the years like the one I had in Ossining that night, I began to understand that many people mask their truest feeling and their deepest wounds. They hide their pain, in other words. And the concealment of it can turn habitual. The pain does come out sometimes, but then it shocks the world.

A delightful and resourceful woman I knew, practical, feeling, effective, smart, and also markedly self-controlled, told me once the story of her long marriage to a man who ceased to love her. They had two fine children. One day, 'out of the blue,' he told her he was leaving her for another woman. They got divorced and lived about ten years of a very frosty connection, almost entirely over the phone, as they stayed in touch concerning their children.

One Christmas, of all days, there was a family gathering, and my friend was there, her now college-age children present, too. Her former husband, their father, was present also. As the lady in question carried a silver tray of hors d'oeuvres from the kitchen into the living room, it just happened, by accident, that she tripped ... over her former husband, whom she didn't see as he was bending over to get something on the floor. Her hors d'oeuvres and dip now splattered all over the floor, and the silver tray clattered loudly on the tile. She herself landed squarely and painfully on her backside. And then it happened. She screamed, and said, "You g-d-mned, f—king a—hole. I hate your guts and I hate everything about you. Don't you ever come near me again. G-d-mmit, if you ever do, I'll kill you. So help me God, I'll kill you." And she sat there on the floor, right where she had tripped, sobbing and sobbing. She didn't stop. The entire house was instantly silenced and completely transfixed.

After almost ten years of silence, this prudent, thoughtful woman had come out with her pain to the highest possible pitch. Had there been a gun nearby at that moment, I think she would have shot her husband, with her children as witnesses and her own mother and father there in the room.

Unanswered Question

Did you ever see a movie called *Journey to the Center of the Earth*? It came out in 1959 and starred James Mason, Arlene Dahl, and Pat Boone. Anyone who ever saw it at the time will remember what the hardy explorers discover at the center of the earth. They discover 6

The aim of this chapter is to help you begin digging to find the root of your main problem in life so it can be unearthed and brought out into the light of God's Grace. The intended result is peace. By that I mean inward peace and tranquillity such that the last third of your life is not consumed by buried but still churning conflict. We seek to quiet the feverish inner sea. This is because churning buried conflict, which lies undiscovered according to a person's outward appearance, can make them vulnerable before their time to heart disease, cancer, and strokes—let alone to terminal outbursts such as the one that overtook my hitherto self-controlled friend and parishioner.

The reason for the digging, for the excavation into the archaeology of your emotional life, is the observation that when buried hurts come to the surface—within the light of compassionate day—they shrink in size and seismic impact. It is like extracting a melanoma. The surgeon tells you after the procedure, "Boy, you should have seen it. It was the size of a lemon." Or, "You'll never believe it. Your tumor was benign, but it was the size of a baseball!" It had to come out. "Either it stays, or I go"—which is to say, either the subcutaneous psychic pain goes, or I die! You really have no choice.

Problem Solving

We were in a Centering Prayer group recently at our church and the accompanying text for our series was entitled *Sacred Rhythms* by Ruth Haley Barton. The book was published in 2006. I was only there for the last session. Normally my eyes would glaze over when faced with a book carrying that title. I mean, I've lived, it seems like my whole ministry, under the shadow of ... the New Age. The word "sacred" and the word "rhythm" in this context—both were sufficient to turn me off without prior notice.

Nevertheless, I went to the group, and it turned out I was woefully wrong. I was in fact hit between the eyes by the author's main contention and felt humbled and a little ashamed that I had dismissed her excellent, insightful book.

Barton posits that every person, and she means every single human being on earth, is involved in a highly individual and most personal struggle to *solve a problem*. Each person's struggle is their own, which is to say there are innumerable problems and versions of problems, and everyone has their very own. But whatever your problem is, you have got to solve it.

Examples of a distinct and lifelong problem that requires solving might be:

> Why was I born from *that* set of parents?
> Why did *he* have to be my father? Or *she*, my mother?

Why was I made to *look* the way I do?

Why was I handicapped in *this* particular area?

Why does no one really seem to like *me*?

Why was I born poor but sent to a school where everybody else was rich?

Why was I born rich but sent to a school where everybody else was poor?

Why do I have such a hard time making myself understood?

You get the idea.

So I am asking you, dear Boomer:

What problem were *you* born to have to solve?

You may have not solved it yet. (It would be unusual, and quite splendid, in fact, if you had solved it during the second third of your life.)

Many people never solve their main problem.

Or rather, many people don't even come close to naming their problem in that sense, i.e., putting their finger on what it is that is really bothering them, until or unless the *static* has begun to soften from the busy second third of their life. That is because the second third of one's life is almost always filled with engrossing static. Few people actually 'stop and smell the flowers.' Many neither look around them nor within them. Other things have captured their attention.

The original problem is there all the time, and it sometimes comes out—in adultery, in sudden, impulsive career switches, in criminal temptations, and in nervous breakdowns. But it more often gets papered over, or displaced onto a patching, quick-camouflaging disguise.

In the last third of life, the un-solved problem of your life, its over-hanging question, becomes harder to evade.

You *can* evade it. You can continue your previous search for professional endorsement. You can continue your attachment to your children by transferring it to your grandchildren. You can just keep climbing up John Bunyan's "Hill of Legality" (i.e., Performance Mountain). But doing so, evading the question, becomes a little harder. Your body is changing and your mind is going. At least to some extent. You cannot run—in place—the way you used to.

When I watched the video of Ruth Haley Barton stating simply and without flourish that every person has a question with which to wrestle, perhaps their whole life long, and that everything you do on a given day ought really to be undertaken in the hope of finding, developing, and using whatever tools you can find to *answer* your question, my brain agreed with my heart: She is right, and she is telling the truth.

"Working in the Coal Mine" (Lee Dorsey, 1966)

Taylor Caldwell is a novelist I admire. She was an outspoken conservative in a period when the overwhelming drive of cultural mores and values was cranking in the opposite direction from hers. She was also an assertive and perceptive Christian. The religious element in life comes through loud and clear in almost all of her books.

What I admire most about Taylor Caldwell, however, is her insight into people. Her characters, both the men and the women, are wrestling all the time—notwithstanding constructs of worldly success and machination taking place around them—with their inward selves. This wrestling is typically brought to the mat, within her stories, in the context of marital crises, and almost just as often in the context of extra-marital crises. Caldwell understands the fluctuating or mobile connections between men and women to be the major arena of emotional de-compression, compensation, and especially *release and healing*.

A late novel of Caldwell's is called *Bright Flows the River*. It was published in 1978. *Bright Flows the River* concerns a successful middle-aged man who has had a complete mental breakdown. He is so ill that he has closed himself off 100% to the outside world and has decided to say not a single word to anyone ever again, not to his wife of 27 years, nor to his children, nor to his two earnest and well-meaning psychiatrists, nor to his mistress—who is the one person it turns out he really loves—nor ... to anyone. A little like Charles Foster Kane, the reader finds out that Guy, this suffering, tortured man, has many reasons that have caused his life to stop cold, or rather, his relation to all relationship, to stop cold. Through several flashbacks, the 'quilt' of Guy's stopped life is gradually pieced together.

The main point of the book, which the author emphasizes almost to the point of distraction, is that the hero's pain revolves around one single question. His question has to do with the nature of love and the nature of God. More concretely, the question has to do with the choice he has never been able to make between the aggressive free-spiritedness of his father and the moralistic Pharisaism of his mother. The poor man is caught between the two conflicting personas of his parents, and he cannot make up his mind as to who he, their adult son, is to be and to become. What I like about her set-up is that Taylor Caldwell writes true to life. Many persons *are* a kind of aggregate mystery, to which there is in fact a single key but it lies buried. It is buried characteristically in the distant heartache-past of their childhood and at the location of a disrupted connection.

How do I know this? I don't know it in the sense of a "categorical imperative," a principle of action or reaction that is true in every case. But I know a few things from my own past. I also know that one or two tools or insights—and more important, a few people, such as Dr. Frank Lake and Pastor Paula White—have excavated a space pretty close to my 'buried treasure' of core pain, bringing it almost or in part to the light. In one case, that of Paula White, she got right there—not a single millimeter away from the primary wound, but right there, on top of it! Talking to Pastor Paula was like Luke Skywalker hearing from Obi-Wan Kenobi at the climax of *Star Wars*, when the Force helps Luke to find the precise but minuscule point of access on the surface of the Death Star into which he is able to fire his victorious rocket.

Let's talk now about excavation. I have affirmed the teleological force of one's personal archaeology and I believe it is the truth of human nature's slavery to compulsion. So let the excavation begin. We are in the Valley of the Kings and are digging for mummified human remains.

The Listener (1960)

You are digging for the root of your own chronic unsettledness, which in turn is the repeating inward disturbance caused by an unanswered question. The diagnostic presumption is that almost everyone carries such a disturbance and that the disturbance is embedded within you, like the churning hot-house ocean in *Journey to the Center of the Earth*. The disturbance is inextricable from everything else that is vital inside you. The point of origin for the disturbance lies in the past; and, because the origin felt painful in the extreme, at the time, at least, when it was suffered, it was quickly buried and covered over. It was too painful to consider, look at, or think about ever again.

Your 'cave burial' of an incident or episode of primal pain is hard to locate. You yourself, in whose body and memory the burial place sits unremembered, have probably long ago forgotten—but really haven't—the spot. But here's the thing—a phrase I try not to use although it has become ubiquitous from pundits on every side of any issue: Here's the Thing. You haven't really forgotten the location of "The Clan of the Cave Bear" (Jean M. Auel), that Paleolithic place of dismembering hurt that underlies every cry and every sorrow to which you have ever given voice.

The 'thing,' in other words, is that people often do know the location of their "Hurt Locker." All it takes for you to bring it to consciousness is to be un-threatened enough, and 'comfortable' enough—another cliché that works—to let your mind scan the inner landscape and find the Luke Skywalker point of entry to the unnatural Death Star that your pain has formed around the original wound.

Gerald Again

A pole, put high enough on a dark night, will suddenly appear shining white in the high dark, because it is intercepting the beam of a searchlight passing over, but otherwise unseen, in the clear dark air.

(H. F. Heard, *Doppelgangers*, 1947)

Gerald Heard's prophetic contributions to human analysis and observation never fail to astonish me. Here (above), in a short but dense work of science fiction entitled *Doppelgangers*, Heard draws us a map for locating the heart of the matter, the locus of dimly remembered but still feverishly active pain.

Heard understands that pain is a pole which is actually sticking high out of the ground even though the night—which is the unconscious mind bearing unconscious pain created in the past—hides it. But we, you and I, have a scanner! Our activated memory, in search of discovery and healing, is the searchlight. It is a little like the alien spacecraft's piercing white light that pinpoints "Wichita Lineman" Richard Dreyfus in his repair truck out on the lonesome highway in the middle of the night in *Close Encounters of the Third Kind* (1977). Our inner searchlight scanning for pain can in fact discern its dark pole. After all, the pole is high, and there is nothing actually covered up about it. Although at night it is "otherwise unseen," our scan can make it "suddenly appear shining white."

It is actually not hard to see and discern the dark pole.

All it takes is The Listener.

Your Answer Is Inside You, Though It's Not Obvious Exactly Where

I used to roll my eyes when people would say, in a song or in everyday conversation, "Just know that your answer lies within. If you look courageously and attentively"—or 'mindfully' (Heav'n forfend—that word!)—"you cannot fail to find the answer you are looking for. In fact, it is *already there*."

It was just that I knew too well what was inside me. I was one of *The Incredibly Strange Creatures Who Stopped Living and Became Mixed-Up Zombies* (1964). (That is a real movie by the way. And what is more, I saw the preview for it on TV in ... 1964! Uncharacteristically, my mother would not let me go see it in the theater.)

What I mean is, what I saw inside me was an inward confusion of disparate elements, some humbly and intently longing for real one-way love, others utterly self-absorbed and only desiring instant gratification. The advice to look within for my bellwether seemed facile: "All you need to do is look inside, trust yourself, follow your heart."

The Dorothy character in *The Wizard of Oz* was played by Diana Ross in *The Wiz* (1978). This was how she sang her wisdom, a partial wisdom in my opinion:

> Believe what you feel
> And know you're right, because,
> The time will come around
> When you say it's yours.

I loved that movie when it came out. But Dorothy's song at the end seemed lame. What was so good about *me* on its own terms? Where was the evidence for this? What I seemed really to see looked more like anxiety, nearsightedness, and sin. It is as though I wanted to add a marginal note **in bold** to the lyrics of her touching song. This was my note:

> Have mercy upon me, O God, according to thy lovingkindness: according to the multitude of thy tender mercies blot out my transgressions.
> Wash me thoroughly from mine iniquity, and cleanse me from my sin.
> (Psalm 51:1-2)

Even so, like many other partial truths, there was *something* inside Dorothy's song. Now I think I know what it is:

Listening as an End in Itself

When someone who cares about you listens to you—doesn't interrupt you, interrogate you, interpret you, nor visualize you through the mirror of their own experience, but just simply and really listens to you—a lot comes out. The surprising thing is that if and when you are really listened to—it seldom happens—*most* of you comes out. And if someone listens to you acutely and well for a long time, almost *all* of you comes out.

That, dear Boomer, is when your archaeology stops being your teleology. That is when your past stops determining your future. That is when you are suddenly free.

In her 1960 novel *The Listener*, Taylor Caldwell again got it exactly right. She posited a small marble Classical building, in appearance like a mausoleum, within a medium-sized Midwestern city, to which afflicted persons of all shapes and sizes, histories and descriptions, all *identities*, in other words, can come, often not knowing exactly why they have been drawn. Once inside the building, each one begins to feel listened to. They never see the person or agency listening. In fact, they never hear a voice nor receive any *words* whatsoever. But there is an empathic presence in the place. And once that presence is felt by the sufferer, who is the Bible's "stranger that is within thy gates" (Deuteronomy 31:12), the person spills the beans. The process may take a while, though sometimes the avowals flow immediately. But everyone, literally everyone—with one exception, that of a person who has come under false pretenses and with evil intent—ends up finding their 'inner man,' their true self. And in the finding, or rather, in the expressing of who they are, they also find the answer to their acute life's question.

Whether it is an 'old-biddy' type of society matron, an angry college sophomore, a burned out Protestant clergyman, a thwarted and cynical 'career woman,' or a dear exhausted family man who makes his living as a plumber —"The Listener," just by listening and by listening only, gets to the exact point, the point of decisive, potentially terminal entry, that Luke Skywalker discovered as he 'lit' over the surface of the Death Star. But instead of the vital opening of the person being the entry to their termination, the vital opening in these cases is the occasion of healing, awakening, and metamorphosis.

Why Good Listening Almost Always Works

I have said that romantic love—not love in general, but the rare and priceless connection of romantic love—is the pearl of great price in many people's lives. That statement should probably be strengthened to read, romantic love, even if thwarted, is the pearl of great price in everyone's life. The reason I posit this as a core truth is not because *eros* is the Greatest Love in itself. No, I posit this as a core truth because within the romantic union of two souls exists the strongest connection we know that can exist inside lived experience. Two souls that were created to have union now have it, albeit temporarily. In other words, the "union of heart, body, and mind" that the Prayer Book talks about in the marriage service is a unique place of truth wherein and whereby a person exposes his or her entire self to the surveillance of another heart, body, and mind. That ineffably comforting exposure is ideally the end and the goal of the coupling. And within that relation, you are intended to be able to express yourself in your entire actuality. "We Have No Secrets" (Carly Simon, 1972).

These are not just words. Anyone who has felt completely and unconditionally in love with another person understands that the relation evokes one's true self. And the evoking includes all of you. At least that's what you want. You want to tell the other person everything about yourself. There are actual moments when you present to the other *the truth, the whole truth, and nothing but the truth.*

This is why I stress—and some propositionally theological people are skeptical of the point (until I ask them how it has been with *them* and they start blushing and become tongue-tied)—that romantic love is the best vehicle we have for digging below the surface to the ancient but hitherto un-accessed buried cave of the worst hurt you ever had. And that is the element in you, "aye, there's the rub" (*Hamlet*, Act Three, Scene One), which lies dormant in every person and is "Cryin' To Be Heard" (Traffic, 1968). It is the cry which in the last third of life, and especially near the very end, becomes, finally, deafening.

The Tommyknockers (1987)

Stephen King published his only alien-invasion novel in 1987. It is a terrific read and concerns a partially recovering alcoholic writer who gets caught up in a battle for the soul and mind of the world which begins in the small town of Haven, Maine. Believe it or not, the writer-hero wins the battle, and wins it solo!

But the novel begins, as most big things do in a person's life, with a tiny, seemingly inconsequential event. The writer's girlfriend trips over a half-inch metal fragment that is sticking out of the ground while she walks her dog in the field behind her house. The fragment looks a little like the end of a can-opener.

Bobbi, which is the girlfriend's name, becomes curious about this metallic 'shard,' you could almost say, and starts to dig around it. Gradually, very gradually, it turns out that a vast interstellar spacecraft, about 100 yards in diameter, maybe larger, is buried beneath the field. Within the craft, too, lie buried the bodies, and more importantly, the dormant minds, of its original pilots. They are not, as in *The Day the Earth Stood Still* (1951) and *It Came from Outer Space* (1953), benign visitors. Rather, they are malignant, controlling, and diabolically unscrupulous.

The analogy is that our buried hurts and covered scars, like the massive underground saucer in *The Tommyknockers*, are often huge down deep, like the tumors I mentioned earlier, "as thick as a lemon," as "big as a grapefruit." In the second third of life, these underground vastnesses and fastnesses of bewilderment, pain, and anger are often drowned out or masked by the 'static' of so-called purposeful living—work, family, 'balance' (a chimaera!), maybe just survival. But in the *last* third of life, when the absorbing intentions of what we believed was defining and important are either softened or dulled by professional retirement and our children's leaving home, then the inner vastnesses have less to hold them down and keep them buried. They begin to poke out. They begin to press against our skin from underneath it.

Good listening, empowered by the listener's empathy of feeling, has the unique potential for getting your pain out, for getting you to 'sick it out,' in such a way that the bind it has on you loosens. In addition, when the primal pain starts to come out, not only does its present hold on you relax; but often it begins to appear, in the light of day, to be not quite the terminating fiery goblin you thought it was. Its hold gets loosened, by means of exposure to the light. Its power—both in itself and in the power you have been giving to it in your mind—diminishes.

Once I was telling a spiritual counselor a supposedly deep dark secret about my father's distant past that I only found out about in my mid-30s. This was the 'big secret' that had been hidden from the children for many years. The man to whom I was telling this, in the more or less immediate aftermath of my having learned about it, let out the casual observation, "Well, *that*'s not such a big thing, Paul. Many families have gone through *that*."

As soon as he said it, concerning what had come as genuine news to me, at least emotionally, I completely relaxed. Not only had the "thing" finally come out—the buried extra-terrestrial craft 100 yards in diameter—but it actually wasn't a hundred yards in diameter at all. It was about 30 feet in diameter.

Opened Ears for the Sake of Personal Peace during your 'Last Lap'

What takes place during the encounter of really being listened to? What is the curative 'agent' within that encounter which works to such benefit?

Notice that I am not asking *you*, dear Boomer, to become a better listener. Such an 'ask' would be an instance of "the law" in the theological/existential sense of the term. In other words, if I were to enjoin you now—if the bottom line of this commendation of listening and its healing dynamic were to persuade you—to become a more effective listener, that would amount to just one more piece of advice. Although it would probably be true, as almost anyone can benefit from becoming a better listener, it wouldn't help you one bit to accomplish the goal.

I can point out to my acquaintances who are terrible listeners that they are just that. But all it does, at best, is shut them up ruefully for a few hours; and at worst, make them never want to see me again. Telling someone to be a better listener doesn't carry with it the power to make them become one. In fact, it will probably just hurt their feelings.

No, the graceful way to go—the only way to get anything done, really—is to ask a person how it feels when *they* are listened to. When Mary Zahl conducts a listening workshop, she often deploys that question near the start: How does it make you feel when *you* are listened to?

Mary's question has a wonderful effect. Almost everyone just lights up with an illustration of a time when they were down and someone listened to them and really heard them. The experience of having had it done *to you* opens the door to the hope of doing it for someone else.

When You Are Heard

The word "abreaction" is a technical term within the practice of psychiatry, but it is a useful one. Abreaction is the term for what happens when your suppressed emotions are enabled to come to the surface and be felt. Previously tamped-down—previously slammed-down!—feelings are expressed; and the expression involves tears, and sometimes anger, too. Didn't Bette Davis warn her guests before a dinner party with her friends who were Broadway stars to "fasten your seatbelts. It's going to be a bumpy night" (*All About Eve*, 1950)? Abreaction is a bumpy ride, both for the emotional 'patient' and for the witness/listener. For abreaction to take place, both the speaker and the listener have to alter the terms of their 'normal' emotional discomfort (i.e., *Moscow Does Not Believe in Tears*, 1980).

When a person is holding onto pain from the past that has not been processed or even acknowledged, that pain is bound to surface with powerful external effect and affect.

Once, an elderly lady we knew, who lived alone in a small New

York City apartment, was injured severely and thrown into a state of clinical shock when, during a heat wave, she opened a can of peaches that had been sitting forgotten at the back of a kitchen cabinet for about five years. As the lady started to open the can, it suddenly exploded! All the peaches literally blew through the small opening she had made, and hit her as well as every wall and surface in her tiny kitchen. She had to go to what was then called St. Vincent's Hospital and be treated for shock. Also, her entire apartment had to be re-painted. The instantaneous titanic geyser of *de facto* pureed canned peaches was so high-pressure that it even reached her tiny bedroom and bathroom. A year or two later, she died in that apartment, and I was there when the police and superintendent had to break down the door in order to find her. There were still signs of peaches on the walls.

Something like that exploding can of peaches is what can happen when crushed and buried pain is given 'permission' to get out. The power of the release is in proportion to how long the material has been hidden and how much pressure has been on it inside.

A person who is abreacting can sit there and cry (and cry) for a full hour; or better, for a full day; or better than that, for a full six months! As Blue Magic sang in 1974, "See the man who's been cryin' for a million years, / So many tears."

The good news is that you almost always feel better and more peaceful after the abreacting release of the feeling. It has been pent up for too long. As the Byrds sang in 1965, "I'll Feel a Whole Lot Better (When You're Gone)."

A Simple Theology of Abreaction

The empathic listener is grace in action. He or she is "one-way love."

The person being listened to is the recipient of grace. The suppressing hammer of the law has caused their deep-seated distress to be shut up tight as an almost automatic response to the pain it caused. The idea of that pain being exposed is threatening—to a person's conceptions or narratives about his life, to his self-regard, or simply to his sense of present contentment. The poor human being reasons to himself, *This suffering is too much for me. Therefore I won't think about it again. Quick, let's fasten down a curtain over it so it can be invisible forever.*

As we know from experience, nothing that has been covered will not eventually be uncovered (Luke 12:2). And according to the lengths we have taken to cover it over and the time that has elapsed since the masking first took place, will be the degree of the explosion when the 'thing' comes out. Even so, the healing can be as instant as the explosion.

One-way love enables the problem to be exposed.

And once the exposure has taken place—in the context of empathy, never of interrogation—it is almost as if it ceases to exist. That is when the mind of the previously suppressing person, her mental attitude and self-imposed narratives, her balance of pessimism, on the one hand, and false hope, on the other, begin to shift. It can all happen very fast.

Grace in relation to the distresses of childhood and youth, which are often covered over again and again, repeatedly, by the static inherent in the *second* third of your life, can have its way with you in the *last* third of your life. Usually not until then do the distractions of life, the static, begin to recede in their intensity. Thus the very recession of your career, your children, and whatever compensatory interests you had chosen for yourself—these 'low tides' provide the opening for your healing. And if you can find someone to hear you out, then their "Thrill Is Gone" (B. B. King, 1970). You can find your right and true mind, your right and necessary peace. The abreaction that comes through graceful listening can do this.

But There's One More Thing

Listening is the main curative in a sufferer's bringing out and feeling the buried pain of life. As Taylor Caldwell recounts so perceptively in *The Listener*, being heard in the presence of non-judgmental love creates a kind of spontaneous combustion by which the pain of the past is drained of its paralyzing hold on you, and your mind clears, sometimes instantly, and you become able to see what steps you need to take next. The past is converted into an acceptance that is almost energizing. The chains that have held you back from a hopeful, positive attitude to life fall off. This happens again and again.

I remember the day and the moment in Nottingham, after having been listened to intensely for about four straight hours by Dr. Lake, who had allowed geysers of feeling to come out of me without any sense of threat to himself, when I emerged from his consulting room and for the first time in many weeks could see the colors of the June flowers in his garden. The day went from black-and-white to technicolor. It was the exact opposite of the Rolling Stones' track from 1965 entitled "When Blue Turns to Grey." Stultifying darkness, in my case, had turned to all the colors of the rainbow. No one *told* me to "smell the roses," but I could—and did.

When I write that, it sounds like a cliché. But it really happened! But there's still *one more thing*.

An Arresting Aphorism

In *The Tommyknockers* the problem facing the town of Haven, Maine, which becomes a problem facing the entire human world, is the implacable mental malice of the dormant aliens within the buried spacecraft. 'Leaning in' will absolutely not do it, for the aliens have only one settled intention, which is to master and control every living thing on the planet. The aliens prove unscrupulous—the word is almost irrelevant to their utterly *other* 'programming' to dominate and exploit. The problem the aliens represent, in other words, is insuperable.

There are some problems—cyclical, suppressed disturbances—which are bigger even than the healing power of listening. Every minister and priest learns that there are some urges in people, some desires for restitution, some deflating inward messages, some inciting inward messages, some passionately felt personal 'issues,' that are resistant to the best and most empathic listening and pastoral care in the world. I am not just thinking of psychotic axe-murderers. I am thinking of people I have known for whom the pain and disappointment of their lives seemed impossible to overcome, or even mitigate.

This was put into memorable words by a woman I knew who was extremely smart and delightfully self-observant, but who commented, after I had told her about my experience in England with Frank Lake, "It would take more than Frank Lake to pry *me* open." She revealed a lot in that remark, for she was a person who notoriously kept her own counsel in the context of a life of airtight prudence, insight, and even kindness. "It would take more than Frank Lake to pry *me* open."

That is why at this point in my own ministry to Boomers, let alone to myself, I feel that necessity is upon us to add something. This addition to my prescription for sustained empathic listening—a hard-to-fill prescription, in any event, for there are not many good listeners in this world—comes in the form of an aphorism from my friend Paula White:

> **What gives you the advantage in life is the supernatural power of God.**

The one *ultimate* arrow in the quiver of hope for persons in pain, the kind of pain that surfaces in the last third of life once the static of the second third starts to calm down, is the supernatural power of God.

Ephesians 6:12

The Apostle Paul saw the negativities of life in spiritual, i.e., unseen but underlying, self-existent terms.

Paul was an empathic listener, as in "the Spirit intercedes for us in sighs too deep for words" (Romans 8:26). Paul was a perceptive understander of persons, which comes through in almost all of his letters to his young churches. Paul also knew about compulsive behavior (Romans 7:15-20). Nevertheless, the bottom line for him in bringing peace and hope to an acutely observed world, was the power of God as victor in the immemorial repeating battle against the devil and his demons. Paul put his view into memorable words near the end of his Letter to the Ephesians: *"For we wrestle not against flesh and blood, but against principalities, against powers, against the rulers of the darkness of this world, against spiritual wickedness in high places."*

I have become convinced of this myself. It is partly why the rather 'moderate' religion in the context of which I have spent over 45 years of ordained ministry now seems, in my final third of life, to be inadequate in relation to the urgent and acute pain of distressed individuals. The old ways work quite well in many cases requiring comfort, presence, and called-for justice. But they don't work so well in a crisis, whether physical, emotional, or pandemic.

'Moderate' vs. 'Intense'

On February 20, 2020, Ericka Andersen published a piece in the *Wall Street Journal* that underlined an important movement in Christianity in the U.S. The article was entitled, "Thank God, American Churches Are Dying"; and was subtitled, "As thousands close across the U.S., lively new congregations are taking their place."

Despite the much touted percentage increase of 'nones,' i.e., individuals who claim to have no religion, within the American population, Andersen observed that there is, going on right under our noses, an underreported *increase* in the percentage of 'intensely religious' persons in our country, i.e., evangelical and especially Pentecostal Christians. In other words, with an increase in 'nones,' many of whom have apparently drifted away from mainline, i.e., 'moderately religious' Christian backgrounds, there is a corresponding increase in those who regard themselves as 'intensely religious.'

Andersen's article did not surprise me, as I have been observing it first-hand for almost 50 years within my own denomination: a gradual but seemingly inexorable "Drift Away" (Dobie Gray, 1973) of the children and grandchildren of those who used to be regular attenders in my parishes. Frequently I have buried a senior member of the parish, whose children, when they arrive for the funeral, evince a quiet but definite hostility towards the religious side of the service. And *their* own children, the grandchildren of the person being buried, are almost always unchurched, having had *zero* religious training in the church of their grandmother. In other words, I am conducting a funeral, and the only practicing Christian in the room is a dead one.

This 'isolation chamber' of religious dead-ness at funerals—the end and acme of 'moderate' religion—became the rule, rather than the exception, in the last parish I served. On three occasions, in fact, at particularly 'W.A.S.P.'-ish funerals in that Episcopal parish, Christianity was explicitly attacked by an adult child of the deceased during a eulogy in church. I had no choice but to sit there quietly and take it; and try my best to 'turn things around' a little at the end.

The Death of 'Moderate Religion' in *The Last Adam* (1933)

In his novel *The Last Adam*, which was published in 1933, the American novelist James Gould Cozzens diagnosed the origins and also the death of 'moderate religion.' He was writing ahead of his time!

At the end of *The Last Adam*, Cozzens gets inside the head of the local Episcopal church's Senior Warden as he is walking in his garden. Mr. Banning, who is a pillar of the small New England town where the novel takes place, and a good man, comes to a sundial, erected and inscribed by his long-dead mother. He begins to reflect on his mother's religious faith, and then on his own faith and that of his wife, Lucile; and, more important for us, on the faith of his college-aged daughter, Virginia:

> Taking up the shears and his gloves, he uncovered the swash let-

ter script encircling the old dial plate: *It is later than you think.*

He was reminded again of his mother, who had placed the sundial ... The inscription had, to her, he knew, a religious value. You were to think how little time remained to prepare to face your Maker, not how little time remained in which to be happy ...

So sure of it all, [his mother] was much less devoted to church work than Lucile. [His mother's] religious relationship was to God, not to the Rector. Only a very rude person would suggest it, but the Church, in its sense of the Episcopal parishes, undoubtedly meant more to Lucile than religion did. She thought of the Church with a comfortable sense of its formal beauty and dignity ...

That was all very well, Mr. Banning could see, but it was not static any more. It would not be the end. Virginia, in a next generation of Banning women, would undoubtedly have no religion, nor any interest in a surviving tradition. At Virginia's age, he could feel intuitively his parents' sober, perhaps smug, acceptance. What Virginia felt would be his unspoken indifference; and little better, her mother's preoccupation with the formal aspects. ... If Virginia went to church, it was distinctly as a favor to her mother and tacitly recognized as that. As far as Virginia was concerned, there was no sense in it. For her to go alone—that was, without any reason—would be unthinkable. Churchgoing was simply a form—fortunately growing milder as she got older—of that adult tyranny to which she submitted because she must. Lucile really would not dare speak to her about God or the teachings of Jesus. It would be safer not to bring up the issue of Virginia's real thoughts and sentiments.

James Gould Cozzens's reflections at the end of *The Last Adam* gave me the breakthrough I needed to understand why, especially in my last parish, I was constantly presiding at funerals in which the only Episcopalian was a dead one. 'Moderate religion' ends in no religion, as Cozzens observed long ago; and that is the cause of 'the nones'.

King Jesus in Miami

On the other hand, during almost 50 years of service in my 'moderately religious' denomination, I would try to get away sometimes to attend 'privately,' as it were, an evening service conducted by T. D. Jakes or a play written by Tyler Perry. There I would be just one among thousands of enthusiastic, 'intensely religious' Christians.

Recently Mary and I visited King Jesus Ministry in Miami, an Hispanic Pentecostal church. We were completely stunned both by the compelling urgency of the pastor and his congregation and by the overwhelming number of people present. The pastor of King Jesus Ministry, Apostle Guillermo Maldonado, believes that God has told him that 10% of the population of Miami will one day be a part of his church. It looks like he is well on the way to making that happen.

The spiritual warfare and immensely positive victory message of St. Paul in Ephesians 6:12 has got to be a part of this message to Boomers. That is because many people carry at least one corroding problem from the first third of their life that not only taints the final third of it, but also proves un-budge-able even in the face of good listening. Something more is needed in order to move the stone of Sisyphus.

Thus this chapter, which was entitled "Digging for the Root of a Peaceful Outcome within a Layered, Archaeological Past," cannot end with the call to even that pearl of almost unlimited price which is empathic listening. As my wound-tight friend said, "It would take more than Frank Lake to pry *me* open." For "we wrestle not against flesh and blood, but against principalities, against powers ..."

In the case of one's worst repeating, presenting symptom, Something More is definitely needed.

"Fruitage"

Mary Baker Eddy's famous 'textbook' to Christian Science, entitled *Science and Health* and first published in 1875, included a section at the end entitled "Fruitage," consisting of personal witnesses from people who had been delivered from illness of many kinds by means of her message. As a young person exposed beneficently to Christian Science, I used to find that section of Mrs. Eddy's *Science and Health,* the section called "Fruitage," a little feeble. The stories involved diseases that had old-fashioned names, and they were told by people that expressed themselves in a style of English that resembled William Dean Howells on a very bad day.

I later came to realize that the point Mary Baker Eddy was making by including these personal stories at the end of her book was to lend credibility to her religious ideas. They were testimonies that were understood to confirm her ideas. Mrs. Eddy's "Fruitage" was a sort of *Guideposts Magazine* digest for the 1880s. "Touched by an Angel"!

Well, let me 'sample' here, in the disc-jockey sense, a paragraph or two of "Fruitage." Or rather, let me channel the impulse.

Towards the end of my sophomore year in college, I went through an excruciating break-up, completely unlike, in its felt severity, anything I had ever come close to experiencing before. Though it probably touched a nerve going back to an early-childhood experience that involved what psychiatrists call "separation anxiety," all I knew at the time was a sense of lyric loss so final that its power overwhelmed me. I did, however, within about four months, bury the thought. I resolved never to think about it again if I could possibly help it.

That break-up, though 'case closed' on the surface and increasingly distant from my real life as it continued, through graduation, marriage, graduate school, years of parish ministry, becoming a father, and right on through to the month of February 2018—the pain of that break-up still had the dormant ability from time to time to 'crop up' or break out from unconsciousness into regular consciousness, especially when other stresses were coming down on me from other aspects of life.

After the death of my mother, the old wound from the distant past started to act up again. There was probably an organic connection between the wound surfacing again and the death of my mother. Let's just say that at this point a 'sunspot' on the sun of my life became inflamed again.

After several attempts to talk about and 'lean into' the youthful pain that had somehow never been healed, I wandered one Sunday into a sermon preached by Paula White, a Pentecostal minister, in Apopka, Florida.

"Brandy (You're a Fine Girl)" (Looking Glass, 1972)

I did not come to hear Paula out of spiritual or psychological urgency, though my problem of the ancient wound was fairly chronic. I came to hear Paula out of curiosity, because she had prayed an explicitly Christian prayer at the Presidential Inauguration in 2017, thereby breaking a taboo that I had accepted since ordination. That is to say, if you were invited, as a local clergyman, to give the invocation at a public meeting or sports event, the only thing you absolutely could not do was mention the name of Jesus Christ. The Name was completely *verboten* in 'the public square.' This was the unconditional 'Thou Shalt Not' of public duty for a minister. Yet Pastor Paula broke it. During her prayer at the Capitol, she broke the inflexible taboo— and not once, but three times.

So I went to her church one Sunday out of both curiosity and admiration.

As Paula was speaking during the service, I suddenly saw an exact and heartbreakingly vivid image of my ancient wound: two young people dressed as for a senior prom. This vision took place with no prompting or expectation whatsoever. It was a stunning and complete surprise, and had no logical connection with the preacher's words. The figures I saw were about 30 feet tall.

One of the figures looked down at me, sitting way below in a metal chair along with everybody else. The figure beckoned in a simple but unmistakeable gesture of farewell. Then the figure dissolved, like a ghost in a movie, dissolving into a thousand particles.

At that exact moment, a song came crashing into my head: I mean, *crashing*. It was so loud that I put my hands over my ears. But it was not coming from the church's loudspeakers. No one was hearing it but me.

The song was "Brandy (You're a Fine Girl)" (1972) by Looking Glass. That song I had not listened to for many years, but it had come out quite soon after the terrible time. It had no direct relation to the persons seen in the vision nor to their story. That was because the song *post-dated them*.

What I was being told by this sudden and unexpected crashing into my consciousness of "Brandy (You're a Fine Girl)" was that I was no longer living in the period before it came out. I was living in the period—really now, the present—*after* the ancient catastrophe. I was no longer locked within a distant trauma that had carried power over me for so long. When I write this, it sounds like a cliché. But that past in its power was over. The song "Brandy (You're a Fine Girl")" was A.D. to my trauma's B.C.

A greater miracle has never happened to me. An unexpected, even breathtaking vision—30 feet tall—followed immediately by a radio-transmission from the distant past, was a stunning surprise. But it really happened, and it will never get out of my mind.

Faith to Move Mountains

My word to Boomers is first to acknowledge the buried 'Mountains of the Moon' that are able, like the chest-bursting alien in the movie *Alien* (1979), to pierce your hopes for a stable rest and a safe harbor in the last third of life. These 'chest-bursters' have the property of being able to lie dormant and still for a very long time. But when the static of money, fame and honor, of spouse, child and career starts to diminish, they have less to contain them. *Sometimes They Come Back* (1991).

This is when listening—real listening, lengthy listening, and compassionate listening—begins to count. Most problems of inner pain can be elicited by means of listening. And then, seemingly without effort—automatically, we might say—the surfaced pain gets transformed into fresh energy and renewed outward-directedness. Acknowledged, surfaced pain almost always creates a new field of compassion within the sufferer. He or she becomes empathic towards others almost to the degree that their own inward suffering has been enabled to come to the surface.

Yet there are some things that are deeper than deep. There are singular matters like my teenage catastrophe, or your childhood psychic injury, that are so grave, heavy, and crippling, that even good listening fails to lighten them and deliver you from them.

It is those things, the deeper than deep, from which only God in His Supernatural Power can deliver you. That is why I told you my story just now.

Let's close with a movie.

Little Boy (2015)

A Mexican production team delivered a first-class A-list movie to the American public in 2015. It was instantly beloved by Christian people that saw it and just as instantly deplored by atheists who saw it. It was not a 'niche' film made for a 'faith' market. In fact, it was a risky work of art with a climax that is probably unique in the history of movies. I honestly believe that *Little Boy* is a contribution to world cinema that is unlike any other.

Little Boy tells the story of a father who must go to war to fight the Japanese at the beginning of World War II. He leaves behind a 9-year-old son, for whom his father is everything. The boy is short and is not getting any taller, so he is the object of bullying both at school and on the streets of the small coastal California town where the story is set. His mother is relatively helpless, emotionally, in the absence of her husband, and her other son is fast becoming a juvenile delinquent with a very short fuse.

One day at church in the local Catholic parish, Little Boy hears the young associate priest preach that if we have but a mustard seed of faith (Luke 17:6), our prayers, including the safe return home of our loved ones at war, will be answered. The child takes the priest literally, goes out and buys a bag of mustard seeds at the local feed store, and starts to pray. Little Boy develops a total focus on achieving his father's return home by means of prayer.

Then it gets interesting. Little Boy is tempted by scoffing local meanies to pray that a nearby mountain would move. It does! (A mild earthquake takes place.)

Heartened by this, Little Boy begins to direct his prayers west, over the Pacific Ocean, towards Japan. He 'hurls' and declaims his prayers day after day, from sunrise to sunset, facing the Land of the Rising Sun, that God would bring his father home.

Behold: Little Boy's prayer is answered. He literally brings the war to an end.

This is as risky a climax as it is possible to conceive. Singlehandedly, Little Boy succeeds in ending the Second World War by means of his repeated prayer of faith.

I urge you to see *Little Boy*. It had an overwhelming effect on my own life. It set the stage for the deliverance I received from Paula White, and I don't think "Brandy (You're a Fine Girl)" would have come over my inside brain-radio if *Little Boy* hadn't first opened me up to the possibility.

And there is more to it even than that. The man who gave me the movie and told me I *must* see it is a man that only God could have put in my path. In no 'normal' or familiar world that would be customary or usual for me to navigate, I met a man selling DVDs outdoors on Union Square in Manhattan, whose gift of this movie was part of what Paula would call a "divine set-up." That man is now a cherished friend, and part of that personal plan of God's which is activated and certainly perceived only through the eyes of faith.

Two Keys to the Kingdom

Let's sum up this chapter so far:

Being listened to rarely takes place. What you observe in the world, at best, is people taking turns talking. And that's on a good day! What you observe most of the time is one person doing *all* the talking. I cannot tell you how many times I am with somebody who is doing all the talking. I've gotten used to it. Would you agree? I probably have to say that at this point in the last third of my life, close to four out of five 'conversations' that I have are one-way treatises, with the other person fully capable of going on for an hour or more without, as we say, 'taking a breath.'

What this reveals is the overwhelming need people have to be listened to. Frank Lake used to say, "Baby the child, so you won't have to baby the adult." Come to find out, many adults were not listened to as children and show it now in their overriding, almost trampling interest in being listened to.

Taylor Caldwell helped us to see this in her parable-novel from 1960 about a listening-room within a small American city, where sufferers feel free to express their worst pain and their most un-met needs.

Therefore, the **first** "key to the kingdom" for finding peace in the last third of your life is finding someone to listen to you. Doing that intentionally, rather than compulsively—i.e., actually locating a good listener and then asking them to hear you out—is rare. I wish it were much, much more common than it is, for the experience of being listened to is foundational. It not only lowers anxiety from the outset, but also seems to elicit and draw out almost effortlessly the foundational pain that fuels so much of the world's heat. Good listening brings forth the suppressed suffering of the entire quenched and frustrated world. I cannot tell you with much confidence to look for it—because a good listener is "more precious than gold, yea, than much fine gold" (Psalm 19:10)—but I can say that without it, you will probably die, as my priest-friend in Ossining almost did, without peace.

Being listened to with love is the first urgent requirement for a good outcome to your life. Think how important it has been within the Catholic Church for a priest to get there in time in order to pronounce the *viaticum* over a dying person. Did you see *The Exorcist* (1973)? Remember the next-to-last-scene, right after Father Damien gave his life to save the little girl; and how his priest friend *did* get there in time to send him on his way in peace? What a powerful scene.

In its institution of required sacramental confession, the Catholic Church has given its members an invaluable resource to meet the need people have to process inner pain and gain closure for it in the interest of their personal, hopeful future. Would that we could all be Catholics in respect to this one Sacrament!

But, yet, I am also holding out for a **second** key to the kingdom. Something has to be brought to bear upon an unfinished life that is even more powerful than listening. This is for two reasons. First, many people never get the chance to be listened to. They go through their whole lives, including its point of termination, without encountering a single compassionate ear. So deafening is the sea of words from other, often intrusive, often manipulative figures, that a person can honestly go forever without an outside person paying un-self-serving attention to them. Thus listening cannot be the only key to final peace, since hosts of people never get within earshot of it!

There needs to be a **second** key, moreover, because *some pain is too great even for empathy*. There are sufferings which consist in "sighs too deep for words" (Romans 8:26). There are cases of an inward wound so painful and also so buried within cancerous over-growth that only Pastor Paula White's aphorism applies to its treatment:

> *What Gives You the Advantage in Life is the Supernatural Power of God.*

You may be one of those cases! Or rather, you may have a hurt inside you that is so embedded and attached that "it would take more than Frank Lake to open *me* up." The pain feels so much worse than even listening could elicit, that you reason, with Hall and Oates, "Some Things Are Better Left Unsaid" (1984).

We under-sell our Christian faith if we do not allow for such cases. There are elements of distress that fester beyond the reach of the best and most compassionate 'horizontal' treatment. That is why 'moderate religion,' as the *Wall Street Journal* article showed, has failed. In at least one case within every life, we need 'intense religion,' which is the vertical Power of God.

For example, you might have, say, four problems presented to you by your past, and it is now, at this point in your life, "When I'm 64" (The Beatles, 1967). As Mr. Banning's mother had inscribed on her sundial, *It is later than you think.* Time is moving rapidly forward. Perhaps three of the 'Final Four' problems from your past have been 'licked'—that is, if you got some help at the right time and were able to pinpoint their location, in memory and inwardness. *But there may be a fourth.*

And that is the one that resists even the most kind-hearted understanding from another. "I just can't get him out of my head" (*South Pacific,* 1949).

The God of the Bible is a Supernatural Power. He is able to break unbreakable chains and cut Gordion knots. Didn't Pope Francis say that his life was saved by "Our Lady, the Undoer of Knots"? Those are not just words. Francis meant them, for he had experienced them. I have seen it take place in my own life. As Pastor Paula says, "A miracle always settles the issue."

So this chapter ends on a high note of hope. Listening works all the time when it takes place, and probably with 80% of life-problems. That is a very high rate of cure. It is like the strongest vaccine to a pandemic virus within human experience. But listening does not work in 100% of them.

"Susan" (The Buckinghams, 1968)

On most mornings my Mary and I take turns listening to each other. The one of us that is speaking sometimes takes a furry ball, the kind that cats like; and passes it back and forth from one hand to the other hand as he or she is talking. That part of our listening is supposed to break down the wall between the two sides of one's brain. Whatever it is *supposed* to do it somehow does. (Don't ask me to explain.)

As I say, Mary and I take turns listening to each other most mornings.

Often the thing that is worrying one of us or stressing us diminishes in its felt power within about five minutes. Although my head sometimes starts to spin—maybe this explains why cats are enigmatic and unpredictable—I always feel better after Mary has listened to me.

Yet both of us also acknowledge that there are some problems from which even listening can't seem to deliver us. There are some situations we face, say, one out of five, that fail to give way even after repeated expressions in words and prayer before the loving face of the other person.

In those cases we have no other choice but to go to God directly. Or rather, we need to emulate our movie friend Little Boy. We need to talk *to* the mountain rather than *about* the mountain. We believe that God can move the mountain that is in front of us and that our faith can move God.

"Not Too Long Ago" (Nick Lowe, 2007) Mary and I both felt done in by an issue we were facing. We had had some real success in lowering the level of worry about it by listening to one another, both at length and in depth. And that left-and-right, back-and-forth furry ball! But the problem itself still seemed superior to the agency and instrument of our mutual listening. It was not giving way.

One Sunday afternoon I attended a service in a field not far from where we live. No kidding, we were 20 people in a field, and the idea was to prepare that very field for a future church plant on the property. (After 45 years of conducting services in cathedrals and so-called 'prominent' city churches, right up to preaching in Canterbury Cathedral, I find myself in a field that used to be a cabbage patch, with 20 dear Christian people of almost every possible ethnicity and human category you could name. Here, finally, I am home. *What Price Glory?* (1952).)

The service was fine, if unfamiliar, and I was touched to be present. But at the end of it, a kind and humble pastor, who had been standing next to me during most of our hour in the field, said, "See that lady over there?" (I had noticed her before.) "She is a great intercessor. She has the gift of intercession."

For some reason, my friend's words got to me, so then and there I went up to the woman as the service finished. I said, "Pastor N. tells me you have a gift for praying for people. Would you be willing to pray for me?"

I won't tell you what happened next, but I will say that the aphorism I keep stressing concerning the Supernatural Power of God proved true and that the prayer-warrior to whom I spoke proved to be, shall we say, highly vertical. I came away convinced that she had directly addressed the mountain of my life rather than just talking about it. Or around it. She had talked to the mountain.

So there are **two keys**, both necessary, both required, both powerful, for the healing of accrued pain. But **the second key is greater than the first.** +++

The Present, Relational Effects of a Settled Past— On Your Children, Your Spouse, and Your Loneliness

I can't help thinking of her lying there alone in the churchyard, she who had never been alone before. And I can't help thinking of the last years of her life, all her money gone, all her brothers and sisters dead, and no one to care at all whether she lived or died. She spent those last years with one of her sons, and they were quiet years. Knowing Grandmother, I feel they must have been a penance for all her sins. Do you remember how she looked when she was dead? Not peaceful or resigned. Just half amused, and—yes, relieved.

(Taylor Caldwell, *Grandmother and the Priests*)

A Good Outcome

Everybody wants a good outcome to their life on earth.

I say "life on earth" because I don't believe our life from the cradle to the grave is all of it. In fact, it is probably just a small part. There is more to come, from a Christian point of view, and therefore a Christian is naturally uncomfortable with phrases like 'the last lap' and 'ending well.' As Dietrich Bonhoeffer said before his execution in 1945, "For me this is just the beginning." Who doesn't desire to see the ending of something intrinsically defeating, such as the physical decline of the body, as "Only the Beginning" (Chicago, 1969)? The atheism implicit in many popular shibboleths concerning "the end of life" is rejected by most people of faith, including this writer.

What we do desire is a sense of satisfaction and even completion. St. Paul wrote at the end of II Timothy, "I have fought a good fight, I have finished my course, I have kept the faith." (4:7) What we very much don't want at the end is dissatisfaction concerning the outcome of our works and days, and the disappointment of early hopes gone unachieved and even scuttled.

Delta of Peace

If the contaminating memories of core pain have been exposed and abreacted in the light of a person's being listened to well, and if the worst wounds have been cured by the Supernatural Power of God— all that is a very big "if"—then a person is living in a state of peace. And peace, "like a river," has distributaries. If you have been listened to well and the inward wounds of your life thus far are being exposed to pure air and salved, then that peace you receive is like the delta of great river. The river bifurcates or 'fans out,' taking its precious water into previously parched areas of your life's Big Country.

The delta of your peace flows into every relationship you have, and especially into your relation to your children, to your wife or husband, and to yourself, "The Lonely One" (Dave Mason, 1970). Not everyone has children. Nor does everyone have a wife or husband, let alone a wife or husband they still love. And even if you do, or did, they may not be alive or present in your old age. In any case, you are alone by definition—everyone flies solo by definition—in your ultimate relation to God. Very few people "die in community," as ecclesiologists often wish to say. That sounds good, as in "No man is an island," etc. In fact, however, judging from experience, you will be fortunate if, like the character of Grandmother in the quotation at the start of this chapter, you even have *anywhere* to go when you approach the end. A great many people die alone.

Right now, however, dear Boomer, you are probably not alone. You probably wouldn't even be reading this book if someone you know hadn't recommended it to you or told you about it. Each of the three distributaries—the channel of your peace as it relates to your children, the channel of your peace as it relates to your husband or wife, and the stream of your peace as it relates to you as an individual before God—is able to flow within and through the lives of most of the readers of this book. And the third stream, the stream unique to you, can flow into the lives of every one of its readers.

The Shape of Personal Peace

Mockingbird Ministries is famous for its focus on God's Grace. Mockingbird Ministries is famous for its delineation, within popular culture and the ethical formation of individuals and society, of the effects and consequences of prior love, and especially the prior love of Jesus Christ, on everyday relationships and interactions. The source of this focus on God's Grace to "Everyday People" (Sly and the Family Stone, 1970) is the New Testament's theology of justification by faith.

The New Testament, and especially the letters of St. Paul and St. John, teaches that people cannot achieve or acquire peace of mind by what they do. Rather, they are on the receiving end of God's prior love, which precedes anything we might do in order to get that love. In other words, "we love because [God] first loved us" (I John 4:19). Therefore, we don't tailor our character and life-performance in order to achieve peace, for that is impossible to achieve given our conflicted human nature and inwardness. Rather, the love of God as embodied in the man Jesus reassures us of our standing and status as valued, precious objects, with the result that our character automatically shapes itself—organically, you might say, and spontaneously— in the ways and directions it is intended to go. One's character and actions, as God intended them to be, are the result of belovedness, not the cause of it.

This result marks the end of effort and stress and the beginning of un-self-conscious, uncompelled outward action. Thus Grace determines character, rather than one's effortful character determining or deserving Grace. The Christian Gospel reverses the customary narrative of working towards one's virtuous growth and ethical participation in the world's life, for love and growth derive wholly from God's *prior* love, or, in the words of traditional theology, God's "prevenient Grace." Everything we do that is actually good we do as the result of being loved and absolved by God in our non-goodness.

Such an understanding of the origin of human virtue is fundamental. God's love for humans precedes humans' love for each other—love, that is, which is any good. The former is unconditional and uncontaminated by self-interest. The latter is inherently conditional and contaminated by self-interest.

Now the peace that is urgently required for a good outcome to one's human life, which we have now seen is a genuine possibility and not just a hope-against-hope, has important effects or consequences in the way you can live during the last third of your life. The peace resulting from abreaction, on the one hand, and direct divine deliverance, on the other, changes the everyday script by which older people characteristically retreat, regress, and go alone toward their death.

Baleful Funerals

During 45 years of pastoral ministry, I have conducted many funerals. At least 10 of these were memorable because of a physical disturbance that took place during the service. Two of them involved a handgun.

At least 20 more funerals I conducted were memorable because of an acute strain of family alienation that marked them forever as 'bad outcomes.' No one who was there will ever forget the main person who was not there, for the reason that her funeral was excruciating.

Let me tell you about two of these funerals.

Once in Westchester County I was called on to conduct an interment of someone I had never met but who had had a distant connection at one time to the parish of which I was rector. When I arrived at the cemetery, which was beautifully located overlooking the Hudson River, there were only two mourners. I was surprised, because I had heard about the deceased, that he was a big success in New York City and had made a lot of money. But as I say, there were only two mourners that day.

After I read the Burial Office from the 1928 Prayer Book, I asked the one man who was there as a mourner why none of the deceased's four sons were present. I tried not to ask the question officiously, but I did feel that something important was not being said. The gentleman turned out to be the estate lawyer for the man I had just buried. He said, sadly though a little sharply, "Well, you see that lady over there? That is Mr. So-And-So's third wife, and none of his sons liked their father. Each of them declined my specific invitation to be here today for their father's funeral. You see, Mr. Zahl, he was a brilliant man, but he was hard on children." So there we were, on a brilliant winter's morning, and the man who had been hard on children was being buried with but one real mourner. And she came and went so quickly that I could barely shake her hand.

Another time, I was called on to preside at a funeral on the eastern end of Long Island. This time there were more mourners and a semblance of 'normality.' Nevertheless, I was told right up front that the person whom the deceased had loved the most in the world would not be there. It turned out that the man's adult son had been arrested in California for drug possession during a strict period in that state when a first offense carried a mandatory heavy sentence. Therefore, this much loved son, who it turned out did *not* love his father, was in the state penitentiary. Even so, it turned out that a week's compassionate leave had been offered the boy in order for him to fly to his father's funeral back east. He could have come, in other words! Yet he had absolutely refused. Here was an exceptional chance to come out of prison and enjoy a week of freedom at home and attend his father's funeral, and he turned it down. So strong was his dislike for his father that he turned the offer down! He would rather stay in prison that week than have a week's freedom back home and attend one short ritual.

What am I saying? I am saying that family relationships are often more strained than they appear, and in the above two cases, which really took place, strained to the breaking point. You may know something about this in your own family. Parents and their children can have un-healed antagonisms—extreme repulsion, to tell it like it is—which get acted out all the way to the end.

The two stories I have told I could repeat several times over. They are not the only such funerals I conducted, not by a long shot. They were vivid instances of alienation so deep that they got acted out, like General Grant's strategy for the bloody Battle of Spotsylvania Court House in 1864, "all the way down the line."

Is there anyone reading this who wants such a thing to happen at the end of your life, let alone right now, during the last third of it, as you begin to wind down and as the prospect of stunted obsequies looms ever larger? What happened in these two instances, one overlooking the sublime and mighty Hudson River and the other at the flowering and fashionable Eastern End of Long Island, could happen to you.

Peace between Parents and Children

If the embedded pain of your life, O Boomer, which came into your system during the *first* third of your life but was fairly covered over by the static intrinsic within the *second* third of it, has been exposed and delivered during the *last* third of your life, then you can have peace with your grown children. This doesn't mean you can 're-do' the incidents and episodes that caused the inflammation to take place within *you* that never really went down, and which may have inflamed the way you brought up your own children. It doesn't mean you can just wipe out or cancel the cutting injuries and hurts that stem from the past actions of your own parents, let alone the injuries you did to your children when they were little. (The "sins of the fathers" do get passed down to the children and to their children's children.) But it does mean that you can become free from bitterness yourself, dear Boomer; and that you can then convey the peace you feel through a mild and un-reactive love that tends to win over the most callused adult son or daughter.

I am talking to you now as the parent in the relationship, not as the child in it.

My wife and I believe we have excellent, loving relationships with our three grown sons. But I am also aware of gaps in my love for them when they were small: judgments I made of them when they were young and impressionable, negative comments I failed to prevent myself from making in my role as father, and rejections that I mostly unconsciously dealt them. So yes, even in 'good' relationships, loving relationships, forgiving relationships, it is likely—almost certain—that a parent will make mistakes, based on his or her own inner betwistings from his or her own earlier life, which will have consequences later.

Yet the peace I am speaking of, resulting from wound-exposure and demon-deliverance, can soften and lessen the anger. Grudges, and we all have them, do not have to be the last word. The man of peace and the woman of peace can eliminate them from their own attitudes, and dis-embitter themselves. Although you cannot change the past, you can change its embittering effects.

I do not believe that anyone reading this wants to or has to end their life with anything like the degree of alienation that existed in the lives and families of the two men I buried in New York. What could have happened is that the tough father with the four sons, who had put his career so far and fatally ahead of their own growing up, could have apologized to them near the end. Even if they had rejected his apology and 'blessed him out' over the phone or in person, one or two of them might well have attended his funeral when the end came. They might have stood stoically in silence, yet it would have helped them to forgive (some) and be present. One of them might have even taken the hand of his step-mother, young and ambitious as they might have considered her, and expressed a little solidarity with her in her husband's death, for she was wrapped in a shroud of total aloneness at his grave.

Similarly, the father of the young man serving his mandatory sentence in a state penitentiary could have written his son a letter near the end. He could have written two letters, or even three. They might not have sufficed to 'make it right,' but they would have gone a ways in that direction. And even if the boy still chose to absent himself from his father's service, the fact would remain that the letters had been written, from a sympathizing dad to his son during the worst period of his son's life.

Peace of mind that is gained when you are in the last third of your life has inevitable good effects on your children. You could say to me, "Well, it is still too little and it's still too late." But it's really not, for the adult child isn't dead and he or she probably has time to process the parent's change of heart. You may be dead, but they aren't.

For the record, I knew a lady from Denmark, South Carolina, whose mother died in a state of particular alienation from her grown daughter. I remember the day the daughter visited her mother's grave for the first time after her mother's funeral. It was about the most painful experience the daughter, who was in her 40s and absolutely wonderful, had ever had. But she did it. She visited her mother's grave. And you know what? The daughter was reconciled to her mother. Right then and there, while addressing her mother in the surrogate form of an inscribed headstone, the daughter abreacted fully, and she forgave her mother. Even post-mortem reconciliation is possible. It's a lot better than no-mortem and forever impasse.

Dear Boomer, write that letter today to your estranged daughter. Call your estranged son. The gesture may not be received well, I realize. You may get the door slammed in your face. But in the long run it is better to do it no matter how it is 'taken.' And you've got the peace now, Boomer, and the Supernatural Change Agent, too, to reach out. You've got what it takes.

How Your End Is Meant to Look and Not Look

The Ancient Greeks knew that the way one's life ends reflects on the quality of one's life up to that point. The ending is not just a last word, it is a summary word. The outcome of your life 'sizes up' the journey that led to it. (I can't believe I just used the word "journey" to describe this mortal coil! If I ever again hear someone say, "It's not the destination, it's the journey," or "The journey *is* the destination," I think I will scream. For it is a false aphorism. The journey that got you there is important, to be sure. The journey that brought you *to* the end has undoubted impact *on* the end. But the *end* is what is important.)

The destination is everything. John Bunyan knew this. Homer knew it. St. Paul knew it, and Jesus knew it. "If Christ be not risen, then is our preaching vain, and your faith is also vain. ... If in this life only we have hope in Christ, we are of all men most miserable" (I Corinthians 15:14, 19). "There's Got to Be a Morning After" (Maureen McGovern, 1973). Everything is intended to tend, despite all disturbance, disruption, and deviation, to an outcome of peace, hope, and union.

What we can say about the 'journey of life' is that the end reflects what came before it. The end sheds light on the pathway that took you to it. You could say that your end is closely conditioned by the degree of peace you won for yourself and ultimately received for yourself prior to it.

This is why the theme of finding peace and hope now, O Boomer, in your last third of life, is vital. If you do, the end of the journey will be serene and quiet. If you don't, the end is likely to be grudging and resistant.

Belligerence

I have been struck in recent Boomer years by the intransigence, even the belligerence of old friends who refuse to prepare themselves for death. People hug to themselves a belief that things will never really change from the circumstances they achieved during the second third of their life. They refuse to admit their physical erosion in heart and mind. They refuse to admit the least 'jostling' by well-meaning people who try to encourage a step such as 'down-sizing' or a timely application to a retirement community.

You may have parents who have made good changes in their situation as they got older. I hope you do. You may have friends who
have been purposeful about the fatal, final third. I hope you do.

But in my own family, and for sure in parish ministry, I have
encountered the 'other half,' the stuck and imprudent half. More
than once, I have accompanied a middle-aged daughter to her just
deceased mother's house, where the newspapers were stacked up to
the ceiling and ancient 72 RPM records were piled four feet high.
More than once, I was told warningly by the adult child of an aging
parent, "There is one subject, Mr. Zahl, that is absolutely unmen-
tionable as far as my father is concerned. That is the possibility of
his ever moving out of his apartment into a nursing home. That is
the one thing that you must never ever mention. It is in-ad-missi-
ble!" Both of the individuals I mention died alone and uncomforted.

For every hopeful and peaceful death—hopefully the ones you
have witnessed or are getting ready to witness, O Boomer—there are
two others you have not seen, which are horrifying. Why not take my
word for it, as a Boomer in the ministry, who has seen the terrible
thing time after time?

Thomas Rowlandson's Impression

The English artist Thomas Rowlandson (1756-1827) was no friend of
the Evangelical revival of Christianity that took place during his lifetime. He was pretty cynical concerning the emotionalism of it. He was
also cynical about almost everything else he observed in his day.

Nevertheless, he made a drawing of a Christian's imminent
death that includes an Evangelical Church of England vicar, the wife
and children of the dying man, and a few members of the dying man's
family. The painting is really a caricature of that profound moment,
a person's death at home in his bed, and the expected weepings and
expressions of last-minute love that would normally accompany
it. The vicar, who seems to be loudly trumpeting Bible verses over

the poor beset man, is delineated as the one leading the goings-on, which appear artificial, almost rehearsed, from top to bottom.

I still like Rowlandson's painting, however, because it shows the importance of the point of departure within that culture. Despite the artist's acerbity of vision, his picture is in painful contrast to the way most people die today. Today most people die in the hospital—despite the best efforts of the hospice movement—hooked up to machines and tranquillized out of their minds.

But this is not an opinion paragraph against 'the American way of death.' It is a further note on the way we are meant to die.

For we are intended to die *in peace* concerning our life's history and *in hope* concerning our future state. The old-fashioned picture of how it should go is not beside the point. For in periods past, the Christian faith was intended to frame our end, the outcome of our life, within these dual confidences of peace and hope. This *Handbook of Hope for Boomers* is about the acquisition of such confidence.

You can see a more serious expression of this Christian framing in any number of Italian Renaissance paintings of a person at the point of death. They depict the dying human being under the direct threat of demons, especially at the precise end of life, attempting urgently to tempt the dying person with doubts about God's future for him and temptations to despair. "Curse God, and die" (Job 2:9). Countering the gloating and tittering demons looking for an opening within the dying person's crumbling attitude and words, is the priest, ever holding a crucifix before the eyes of the pitiful and assailed subject. It is the Supernatural Power of God against the persistent, bewitching beckonings of the devil and his hosts. But the Power of God is greater than the bats and the gargoyles.

My point is that there is always hope for a peaceful, thankful end. Whether you are in doubt about it, i.e., Thomas Rowlandson, or in total earnest, i.e., Duccio and Giotto, your ending is supremely important. So why not anticipate it, take hold of your peace by means of abreaction and deliverance, and live from it now?

Peace in Relation to your Husband or Wife

Permit me the freedom not to use the word "spouse."

I feel under pressure sometimes to use it in order to avoid the more 'binary' terms "husband" and "wife." But I don't wish to avoid the binary. Allow an author who is in the last third of his life to sound a little less than contemporary. Allow me to sound like the Jenny Agutter character, 'Jessica', in *Logan's Run* (1976), who escapes with her somewhat chilly lover from an android/nihilist world, out into the ruins of the once-human world that surrounds it and finds herself captivated by inscriptions in a ruined cemetery that say "my beloved wife" and "my beloved husband." She is moved by these words, and so are viewers even today of that colorful 1970s sci-fi extravaganza. One day, maybe, we'll come back to the mood of such memorial verses, and they will move us again. Right now, I'm with Jessica from *Logan's Run*.

What does acquired Boomer peace look like in relation to your husband or wife during the last third of your life?

Contingency and "The Power of Love"
(Frankie Goes to Hollywood, 1984)

In principle, marriage is the closest relation an adult human being ever has to another. It is undertaken in the promise that it will not end "until we are parted by death." Therefore marriage is subject to the never-ending opposition to it of contingency in human life. We are not given to know the details of what will come against us and in what ways our happiness and life's outcome will be affected by outward circumstances, from the world's turning upside-down occasioned by the coronavirus to every one of the "slings and arrows" you can name of "outrageous fortune." What you promise is to "love, honor, and cherish" the other "until we are parted by death."

The heaviest weights on marriage, however, which is a relationship between two people involving their whole hearts, bodies, and minds, do not come from outward contingency. The heaviest weights on marriage come from depleted love, disappointed self-sacrifice, and the temptation to believe that another, third person can do for you in the core need to be loved what your actual husband or wife cannot do. I am saying that the quality of your love itself, the enduring, mutually inward, renewing bond of intimate emotional and physical intercourse, is the anchor of marriage, not the outward circumstances which accompany it.

The Stream of Peace Within the Last Third of Your Married Life

If, as I have said, the sunderedness of your own psyche deriving from the first third of your life has been exposed in the context of empathy during the last third, and if the worst pain of all has been met by the Supernatural Power of God, then the gift of peace should flow like a river into the most experienced of all life's relationships, which is your marriage. I say "most experienced" because over time the marriage state is the least interrupted, most weathered, and most archaeologically penetrating of all human connections. Your parents, who are older than you, die, often sooner rather than later. Your children, who are younger than you, grow up and leave home. But your husband or wife is usually your contemporary in age, or close to it, and has the strongest chance of staying alongside you of any other person. These are generalizations, and there are many exceptions to them. But for the most part they hold.

What if the walls that separate you from your husband or wife really were to come down during the last third of your married life? Such 'walls' are mostly inward ones. They include deeply held grudges and bitter memories from the first years you spent together—miscommunications and judgments which damaged your well-meaning affection and have never really lost their sting. Their impact is buried much of the time, for sure. But it has the surprising quality of being able to boomerang back and haunt your family home.

You are each very different from each other, and you always were. There were occasions when the 'Venus' in her and the 'Ares' in him stood across from each other in a kind of truce, or even 'phony war.' Such a truce may have gone on for 30 years. It is breathtaking and disturbing, if you have been married for a long time, how hurts and grudges from the first third of your marriage—and maybe just the first five years of it—can come out in a present-day contention with white heat! Old scars can have a long life. In fact, they rarely fade until they are exposed again.

"You weren't there for me when our first child died." "You didn't pick up on my depression when I got fired that second time." "You let me do *all* the scut-work when you were sick, or said you were; and afterwards, too." "You took me for granted when you announced we were moving, for the fourth time!" "You never let me *feel* after we supposedly 'recovered' from the affair you had after our second child was born. You just wanted to pretend it never happened. But it did happen, and you hurt me very deeply!" The beat goes on.

Marriage's greatest 'pandemic' is resentment and suppressed anger based on instances of past rejection and unfairness that have not been acknowledged.

Vaccine for This Particular Virus

Intra-psychic peace has a deep trench through which to flow in the field of your marriage's last third. And during that final third, the phase in which most married Boomers find themselves, the heart of the matter is self-giving love and its longed-for endurance, rather than ever-changing negotiated arrangements concerning shared responsibilities. What I mean by this is that the primary issue in long-term marriages, which all marriages really are in their founding, principled intent, is the quality of the love subsisting between husband and wife. Their 'doing life together' depends on the sincerity and genuineness of their love and its intimate connection, not on the couple's outward circumstances or even their individual temperaments.

Let me put it another way. In 1972 Roberta Flack and Donny Hathaway had a big hit with their song "Where is the Love?" The title of that song asks the enduring core question of every marriage. OK, so we still love each other, but "Will You Still Love Me Tomorrow?" (The Shirelles, 1960).

Marriage in the last third of life is not about habit, nor is it about compromise. It is not about utility, and it is not even about the quantity of years and time spent together. Marriage in the final third is about a unity that is constantly re-created by the still welling spring of romantic love, albeit deepened by shared suffering; and, for people of faith, shared humility in the face of God.

What the healing of hurts from the first third of life is able to accomplish to benefit the last third is fundamental to a good outcome for your marriage. "Love Grows Where My Rosemary Goes" (1970), which is to say, love is sustained wherever the stream of inner peace is able to flow. If you are settled within yourself in relation to your past pain, then you do not have to fight for anything. Your demands are few, and, as it turns out, anticipated by the husband or wife that cares for you and loves you.

We were counselling a couple who were in their mid-30s and bringing up their two small children. The wife, who was herself a psychologist, kept insisting on the necessity of "boundaries" in relation to her husband. It was a mantra with her. She stated about five times, just in the first session, that boundaries were the great, overriding necessity for her being able to stay with her husband. He himself was trying hard to stay married to her, for he loved her, so he tried to take her point.

After that session, Mary and I both said to each other, Why is she making such a point about boundaries? What is she really saying?

We found out. The wife was having a long-term extra-marital affair with someone in a distant city whom she would meet at professional conferences, and she didn't want her husband to approach her physically. "Boundaries" was the word for that natural though unnatural resistance to the man she had married but whom she no longer loved. In fact, the extra-marital relationship, which was the backstory to the couple we knew, had no boundaries at all! The word was being manipulated to build a wall between one couple in order to protect another couple for whom the walls of reserve and taboo had crumbled utterly. The term was covering something fundamental—and fundamentally deceptive.

When the truth came out, the couple divorced.

Even within the second third of your marriage, when the static of schedules and overlapping demands is loud and sometimes deafening, Roberta Flack and Donny Hathaway's song applies. For "when the walls come tumblin' down" (J. C. Mellencamp, 1983), when the boundaries between two married people vanish, then the love which is intimate connection becomes visible again. And in the last third of your marriage, if you and the person to whom you are married are still both alive, the love that has no boundaries flows into the most intimate union. The answer to the song's question "Where Is The Love?" then becomes: Right Here!

The old Gospel hymn "Nothing Between" says it well in religious terms:

> Nothing between my soul and my Savior,
> So that His blessed face may be seen;
> Nothing preventing the least of His favor;
> Keep the way clear! Let nothing between.

That is the heart of an enduring intimate connection.

God desires nothing between Him and us. He only desires unmediated mutual union. Similarly it is the whole sum of what Mary and I desire for ourselves right through to the end: Nothing Between.

"But You Have Saved the Best for Last" (John 2:10)

What greater thing is there for two human souls than to feel that they are joined for life—to strengthen each other in all labour, to rest on each other in all sorrow, to minister to each other in all pain, to be one with each other in silent unspeakable memories at the moment of the last parting?

(George Eliot, *Adam Bede*)

A couple years ago I read that paragraph from the conclusion of *Adam Bede* during a staff meeting at a Pentecostal church I love. A woman older than I is on the pastoral staff of the church, and came up to me after the talk. She said with rich feeling, "Where is that quotation from? That is me and my husband. Where can I find the book?"

It turned out that Elder Marguerite, as we call her, had been looking after her bed-ridden husband for a long while. He could not get out of bed and had to have full-time care whenever Elder Marguerite left the house. In other words, her life at church was being given over entirely to good works and helping sufferers with their problems, while at the same time her life at home was being given over entirely to helping her suffering husband.

Recently, her husband died. Our senior pastor at the church gave this good Christian man a prophetic word at the point of his death, a word of security that he could go to Jesus in peace and confidence. He died almost immediately after being offered that word of hope. Elder Marguerite was herself at peace, and no one could be more thankful than she for her many years of happy marriage.

Dear Boomer, it is possible to have an Emerald-City marriage right down to the end of the line. The love you have now does not depend on outward circumstances nor even on good health. It depends, rather, on the razing of the walls between you.

"Tumblin' Down" (J. C. Mellencamp, 1983)

If you or your husband or wife are carrying buried uranium ore of past grievance and suffering—and you probably both know what I am talking about—the "boundaries" between you are a problem. John Cougar Mellencamp was right. For love to be born, and born again, then born again, the walls need to "come tumblin' down, tumblin', tumblin'."

Often the exposure of wounds and sorrows, and hidden drives and motives, comes out during the first bloom of love, even in your twenties, or your teens. You find someone to whom you feel able to tell everything. Like the Samaritan woman at the well in John's Gospel, you "tell [him] everything I have ever done" (4:29). The release involved—in abreacted exposure of your true self in the presence of someone who loves you without faulting you—is massive. You want to marry them right away!

Almost every marriage starts in the right place, and the right place is un-suppressed truth-telling to another. Later, in the second third of your marriage, the static of arbitrary demands and even self-inflicted worries and burdens drowns out the original thunder and lightning of what got you started. Yet hopefully you make it to the last third of your life's great connection. You are both Boomers now, both retired and a little stunned by the quieter atmosphere of your life. Your children are also grown and have their own lives to govern. What feeds your marriage now?

Well, take it from The Lemon Pipers:

> And when I get older and wrinkles appear,
> Will I still find some rice in my hair?
> ("Rice Is Nice", 1968)

You have to go back!

Remember what Gerald Heard said: "If you want to find God, go back to where you lost Him." Paraphrase this for marriage and you get, "If you want to find love again for this man or that woman, go back to where you lost it"—which was probably during the second and "static" (i.e., as in *The Twilight Zone*) third of your life together. The love *is* there, and obviously *was* there when it all began. But it became dormant, quite un-thermal and fairly distracted.

Two things to do, if I can put it that way. Or rather, here are two things that describe the re-discovery of married love in the middle and late years of your life.

Number one, talk to him or her about the things on your heart, especially your "trouble in mind" (Janis Joplin, 1965). "Tell her about it" (Billy Joel, 1983). If you do so, even if it's just a start, the feelings you have been masking will probably find their right exposure, just as they did back in the '60s when you stayed up all night talking to him. Abreaction will happen, the accompanying diminishing of pain will take place, and your link with her or him will be soldered again.

Number two, pray God to take away the pain you *can't* talk to him about. There may well be a "boundary" between your hurt and its surfacing, a wall between your bitter loss and its release into the ether, let alone towards the other. It may be that only God can sledge-hammer down that wall. I recommend a good healing ministry. Write me and I'll recommend one. I have one I use at that Pentecostal church where Elder Marguerite is on the team. We also have one at our terrific Episcopal church in Winter Park. There is a brilliant healing ministry, known as 'Advent House', connected to Cathedral Church of the Advent in Birmingham. And there are others—not many, but a few. You may need "more than Frank Lake" to pry *you* open.

The marvelous effects of abreaction in the presence of a good listener, and the Supernatural Power of God in the case of nuclear waste buried below the earth: these two dynamics are the secret of a good outcome for a Boomer marriage.

"This Is for All the Lonely People" (America, 1974)

BUT NOT EVERYONE is married.

Not everyone has children.

Not everyone even has friends.

Some people were married, but are married no longer. They are widowed or divorced.

Some people had children, but their children have died or don't care.

Some people had friends, but all their friends are dead.

Many, many people live alone, and especially among the 'demographic' of the late middle-aged and elderly. Many Boomers live alone, or are going to soon.

"This is for all the lonely people."

How Can Single Boomers Find Peace?

Un-accompanied single Boomers—and I expect I will be one some-day, dreadful as the thought is—are able to find peace by the same means that married ones do. They need to be listened to, or they will go increasingly out of their minds. And they need to betake them-selves to the Supernatural Power of God.

I was Rector once of the Episcopal parish in Chevy Chase, Mary-land. The church was on Chevy Chase Circle, on the border between Montgomery County and the District of Columbia. Almost every weekday I would meet a different parishioner for lunch on what is called Upper Connecticut Avenue in northwest Washington. Walk-ing daily up and down that crowded avenue, I cannot tell you the number of single older persons, mostly female, I would pass. The pal-pable loneliness of the legions of solitary, elderly persons dragging shopping carts back and forth to the Safeway could not help but make an impression. Here was the city in which I had grown up, surrounded as a child by friends, teachers, and family. Yet all I could see now, 40 years later, were unconnected queues of atomized "Eleanor Rigbies."

The mental health of the Boomer generation is an extremely im-portant issue. An almost unbearable loneliness and its attendant men-tal depression are chief characteristics of lonely Boomers. People are dragging themselves through life, basically waiting for death. Happy indeed are the married couples who have survived their 65th birth-days together. Happy for sure are the married couples who have adult children that care and actually do call them on Sunday afternoon.

But my focus now is on "all the lonely people."

There are, again—and you won't be surprised when I say it—two curative, sustaining agents for the millions who have no one to talk to. The first curative agent is a listening ear. You can scarcely believe how relieved and delighted a person living alone can be in the com-pany of another person who actually wants to listen to them. You who are the potential listening ear may get rebuffed at first, for the person who needs to be listened to has become "accustomed to her face" (*My Fair Lady*, 1956), by which I mean the face of loneliness, and oddly resentful at first of an interested presence of love. But when the message is received, that you really do care and wish to know what is going on with them, miracles take place.

In the Presence of Ganesh

I was visiting a wealthy widow once on an estate outside Ossining, New York. She said she didn't really want a visit from her occasional rector, who was me, *but* that she had recently rented a cottage on the grounds to an old friend of hers who was a widower. She said, "You go see him. I think he needs you." So I did. Knocking at the door of a charming little house that you could almost see from the main house, I got the response, "Go away, I'm taking a nap." So I did.

But there was something about the situation that seemed to draw a response in me. I went back the following week, and the old gentleman who was living in the cottage answered the door and said, "Sally told me you might be coming. What do you want?"

Well, despite the frosty welcome, I managed to get inside the house. There was a statue of the Hindu elephant-god Ganesh in the living room, and for some reason I asked my 'host' about it.

That was all it took. It turned out that he had served as a consul for the U.S. State Department in India, that he was interested in Hindu beliefs concerning reincarnation, that his wife who had died two years before had been a fascinating person, and that he himself had had a born-again Christian conversion experience exactly one year ago, while living and grieving in California. The man, whose name was Paul Sherbert and was originally from Boston, spoke with Beacon Hill refinement, with cosmopolitan wisdom, and, gradually, as he warmed up, with a kindly twinkle in his eye. Paul was about 80 years old.

Within three months, this good, lonely man became a regular part of our Episcopal church, a pillar of the once-a-month 'charismatic' healing service that we offered on Sunday nights, and one of the best friends I ever had in Westchester County. With me and a few others, Paul came to abreact the core loss of his beloved wife and to ask God for help in counter-acting his resultant loneliness and surface irascibility. Before he died, I would have called Paul one of the most touching "epistles ... written ... in fleshy tablets of the human heart" (II Corinthians 3:3) that Mary and I have ever had the privilege of knowing in all our years of parish ministry.

One Question

All it took to get to know Paul was to ask him one question. That is all it took. The question happened to concern his resident brass 'idol,' Ganesh, the elephant-god from India. That was the first step by which Paul's life would move from desolation to renewed outreaching love. For Paul had a lot to say, and he had already lived a long, interesting life; but he was still in the midst of primary grief for his wife, Alden.

Because of his years in India and all the more so because of the single sundering loss of Alden, Paul was also directly interested in religion. It just happened—this was God's marvelous work—that Paul had paid a companion to look after him, in the immediate aftermath of Alden's death, in his big house at Ojai, California. The companion he hired was an evangelical seminarian at Fuller Seminary in Pasadena. That seminarian, a kind lovely man in his mid-30s, had asked if he could start a Bible study in Paul's house on a weekday evening. Paul had said yes. About two months into it, Paul himself started to attend, for he was very lonely. The sincere and embracing love emanating from the members of the Bible study caused Paul to want to become a Christian. So he did. The Paul I met just one year later knew the Christian Gospel, mixed it delightfully with some elements of Indian religion, and applied it as best he could to the still extremely tender loss of his wife.

After he had moved cross-country to Westchester County north of New York City, Paul lay there in his small, attractive cottage most afternoons, open with raw and searching heart to whomsoever God put in his path. It was then that his landlord sent her minister, whom she barely knew, to Paul; and it was then that Ganesh inspired my innocent question.

"I have one gift. I listen to people."
(Thornton Wilder)

Boomer, find a good listener, especially if you are all alone. Good listeners are few and far between, but they exist. There may be one next door. There is probably one at church.

Now maybe you have tried. Maybe you have tried to find a good listener and were disappointed. Many people have told me about the time they went to their pastor or priest with a problem, and the minister just talked about himself and his or her experience rather than listening to—hearing out—the person who had come bereft. Some have even said that they resolved at that frustrated point *never again* to reach out to the Church. So yes, maybe you tried and failed. There was no good listener available to you.

Yet there is an old maxim that may cover this: "When the student is ready, the teacher appears." In other words, if you really, *really* are seeking a wise counselor, and perhaps asking God to lead you wherever He will, there is probably someone who is at this moment rounding the corner in your direction. No kidding. Sincere faith almost always finds its answer, its healer, its compassionate friend. Sincere faith is like a heat-seeking missile.

But everybody *else*, you take some time now to listen to a Boomer! He or she probably has a lot to say and almost no one to whom to say it. You cannot do a greater service to a Boomer than just to listen to him.

Tears come more easily the older you get, particularly with men. Charles Foster Kane had no one, not a single soul, despite being surrounded by 100 paid staff, to listen to him. He had no one to cry with. Thus Citizen Kane died in despair, wholly preoccupied with his past and unanimously misunderstood.

Boomer, submit yourself also to the Supernatural Power of God. There are memories and patterns within you that you cannot afford to take with you. The bad-to-worst things about your life need to stay on this side of the grave. There are instances of love to take with you, and sunny moments of belovedness that belong to you forever. But the rest needs to stay here! Only the Supernatural Power of God—what Sir Norman Anderson called our "Jesus of the Scars" after the shattering death of his adult son—can separate you from the scuttering roaches and extreme regrets within your past that are buried under a rock not yet uncovered. Find a good church, in other words—they are few and far between, but they exist—and especially a good minister. You need the inspiration that comes from God.

Mary and I love the plays of Tyler Perry. One of them, *Madea's Family Reunion*, was made into a movie in 2006. A crucial character, Aunt Myrtle, who is living out the end of her life in a busy nursing home, is played by Cicely Tyson. We learn all we really need to know about Aunt Myrtle when Tyler Perry's camera, for he directed the movie of his play, first scans her humble bedroom. The most important object in the room is The Holy Bible that sits by her bed.

As the storyline moves forward, we discover that this faithful woman is the hinge point for her entire extended family. She is a woman who relies on the Supernatural Power of God. And it comes out! To the extent that she has been given *to*, she gives out.

Cicely Tyson's character is the icon of a healed and peaceful Boomer. ⊹⊹⊹

CHAPTER FOUR

Felt Gratitude—It's More than Just Words, It's a Welcome Invasion!

The theme of this book began with three podcasts recorded for Mockingbird Ministries in late 2019 and early 2020, concerning the means by which God's Grace, which is to say, God's One-Way Love, creates a successful way to live during the last third of life. The aim of the casts was to encourage the listener with hopes of his or her life's good outcome. Not that I am an authority at age 69, for mostly I have been making it up as I go along. But if a theology of One-Way Love can't help you in your 60s and 70s, was it really as great as we thought it was during our 30s, 40s, and 50s? There has got to be a link. One-Way Love can't date if it is true.

When Mockingbird first began in 2007, the 'petri dish' for its work, the primary context for its focus on God's Grace as the open door to new life and hope for sufferers, was the population known as Millennials. This was the generation reflected in almost all of Mockingbird's founders. It was also the demographic that was thought to be leaving the Christian faith in favor of no religion at all—the so-called 'nones.' Mockingbird was therefore a renewal movement for mainly Millennials. In important ways, it still is that.

So when I recorded some chance podcasts about the message of Mockingbird in relation to people my own age, the 'Boomer' generation, I was surprised by the response. Either we were already reaching more 'Boomers' than we realized, or our 'Millennials' were somehow morphing into 'Boomers' behind the scenes. Or maybe *their* 'Boomer' parents were starting to get their attention. Or—and this was the best possibility—maybe what I was searching to say in those three episodes of "PZ's Podcast," speaking as I was from my late 60s, carried some application to everyone.

I still haven't figured it out, and maybe you can tell me. What I do know is that three words came to the fore—in fact they came to Mary first—as I thought about Boomer disappointments and Boomer exhaustion, Boomer losses and Boomer enervation, Boomer decline, physically, and Boomer grudges against life, Boomer reactivity and Boomer judgmentalism, Boomer limitations and Boomer dread, and especially Boomer anxiety before encroaching illness and imminent death. The three words that came to me and Mary, or better, the three strengthening possibilities for which we found ourselves actively longing, were *gratitude, peace, and hope.*

That sounded possible, so I went forward with the project. There was only one problem, though it was more formal, or semantic, than material, or substantial. I could not distinguish, from within my own life, the experience of gratitude from the experience of peace. Gratitude and peace are not exactly the same, but they act the same! If I become grateful later for a bad experience in life that, at the time it happened, offered no possible reason I could see to give thanks for it, then that retrospective way of seeing it leads almost instantly to peace about it. One's peace was generally disturbed by memories and feelings for which there was no gratitude, but only resentment and anger. Yet if the inner landscape somehow 'flipped,' as we say today, and the negative thing was now seen as positive, well, then the result was peace.

Maybe we can say that peace is the opposite of conflict, and conflict becomes peace when the origin of the conflict is transformed by new understanding into an experience that 'had' to be. So rather than resent "The Bad Seed" (1956), you become thankful for it because it had to be; and that leads to peace.

This could all become a purely mental construct, a form of words, to be sure. But there was also something in it. More than one bad situation in my life had become in hindsight a crucial development in offering me something better. "Is this the start of another heartbreak, girl / Or something better beginning?" (The Kinks, 1965). Or, as Joseph said to his brothers in Egypt, "ye thought evil against me; but God meant it unto good" (Genesis 50:20).

What I observe in these recent Boomer years is that achieved gratitude for things for which I did not feel gratitude in the initial situation drains the conflict away and results in peace. Gratitude is a constituent, or better, a building block, of peace. They go together.

Peace is the *main thing* you want, conveyed through the abreacting power of good listening and the Supernatural Power of God; but the perspective that completes it and gives it longevity in the big picture of your life is gratitude.

Is God One or Is He Two?

An ancient subject within theology is the question of God's monism in relation to the duality of the world He made. Monism refers to the description of God as One, hence the word "monotheism," which typifies religions that reject the possibility of many gods. Christians believe in One God and not in many.

But what about the opposing forces, so visible in the world, that are hostile, cruel, and besetting? Is there another Force at work in addition to God, a devilment? That would make two powers in the world: God and ... whoever or whatever is against Him. Or is there One God and two Forces, but God always wins? Or is the One God somehow limited—does He allow Himself to be limited—by the other, contrary Force or forces?

You could define "monism" as the belief that there is ultimately only one Force, God, and that everything that happens is within His will. You could define "dualism" as the belief that that there are some things—the bad things—that do come not from God, but from some Adversary or Antagonist.

I am both a monist and a dualist in reference to the One God. The statement requires explanation. Moreover, I am both a monist and a dualist at the same time not because it satisfies the rules of logic, which it may do; but because I have seen the One God at work in the many-ness of life and have also called upon that One God to combat the very real adversaries that hate Him and ultimately hate me. As a Boomer, life-experience has made me both a monist and a dualist at the same time.

The question of God's monism in relation to the duality of the world as we experience it is important in connection to gratitude. The question cannot be solved by thinking. Or rather, it *won't* be solved satisfactorily through a form of rational explanation. It is a question that is answered only in the human heart, the seat of our convulsed feelings that has been broken by reversal and misfortune. The *why* of life's ambiguity and tragedy is related intimately to the reality, if it is a reality, of God's monism, on the one hand, and the world's dualism, on the other, and how these two are connected.

What I am saying is that the theological paradox of monism and dualism has to be resolved finally within our own experience. And the older you get, the better I think you are fitted to see it. The last third of life gives something like clarity on this, after the second third of life has muddied the water confusingly and even despairingly. Boomers, simply because of their chronological age, have an advantage in solving, or rather, accommodating themselves to, the paradox of monism and dualism.

"This is the way it had to be"

It was Dr. Tom Calhoun in Denver, Colorado, to whom I dedicated my first book for Mockingbird, entitled *PZ's Panopticon*. Dr. Calhoun used to say, when I opened the book of my life and read chapter and verse from what I saw as its rejecting, dispiriting pages, "This is the way it had to be." That was a monist view, and it proved immensely comforting.

Take out the "red book" of your life's story. There are at least three and probably more serious deviations from what you expected to take place. There are probably about five very questionable decisions that you made. A couple of them were mis-judgments of people, a couple were false starts in relation to career, a couple may have been mistakes with money.

The worst mistakes you made, the ones that left the most lasting impression and deleterious marks on your own skin, had to do with people. Any one of those errors, had you avoided making it, would have made a big difference in the way your life has gone.

You also made mistakes in evaluating yourself. You thought you could do something that it turned out you couldn't. Or you failed to do something important by underestimating your potential. Yet to all that, Dr. Calhoun replied, "This is the way it had to be." I took heart from that.

But this one came from the Pit!

Yes, I took great heart from Dr. Calhoun's monism.

At the same time, though, I also saw in the origin of the bad things that had happened to me, or perhaps their 'motive,' if I can put it that way, a malignant opposition to my person and my hopes for happiness.

On the one hand, an unhappy, broken relationship in adolescence proved to be the pivot-point to a happy relationship, a lifelong unbroken one, in early adulthood. And a mid-career misstep proved to be the 'diving board' for a more fulfilling and appropriate billet later on. In hindsight, a defeating experience, which had been misconceived from the start, set me up for something more satisfying in the long view. What had been "meant" for ill, God used for good.

Behold, a mystery! The very thing that not only hurt me but puzzled me, turned out to be the occasion for a change that blessed me. This happened more than once.

Pastor Paula has an aphorism that expresses in the present tense the experience of hindsight I am talking about. She writes,

> *All that seems bad in your past is working for good in your future if you allow it to!*

These words make Paula a monist. Note that she does not deny the 'badness' of the past. She just envisions a Good Hand, an ultimate benign causation, behind the badness.

"This is the way it had to be."

The Welcoming Prayer

Mary and I take part in a Centering Prayer group that meets weekly at our Episcopal parish in Winter Park, Florida. The main founder of the present-day Centering Prayer movement was Father Thomas Keating (d. 2018), a Catholic priest. Fr. Keating is usually credited with "The Welcoming Prayer," which is a pure statement of the monism of God:

> *I welcome everything that comes to me today*
> *because I know it's for my healing.*
> *I welcome all thoughts, feelings, emotions, persons,*
> *situations, and conditions.*
> *I let go of my desire for power and control.*
> *I let go of my desire for affection, esteem,*
> *approval, and pleasure.*
> *I let go of my desire for survival and security.*
> *I let go of my desire to change any situation,*
> *condition, person, or myself.*
> *I open to the love and presence of God and*
> *God's action within. Amen*

Thomas Keating's prayer is a no-holds-barred, unconditional statement of the monism of God. It affirms that "everything that comes to me today" is for my good. It is meant to be. This is a staggering belief, and one that is able to cause whole swathes of a person—whole swathes of the human race—to stumble over it initially and react almost instinctively against it.

We came to know well a couple late in the second third of their lives whose daughter had developed serious mental illness in her early adolescence. The young girl was hospitalized for a long period and could hardly have been more afflicted in mind.

Once when I foolishly commented that the parents' severe affliction, i.e., their daughter and her illness, might in some way be connected to a larger purpose, i.e., to God, the mother exploded. She was a 'Southern lady,' and the explosion, which came during a dinner party, was out of character. Very, very sharply she said to me, "What kind of God is it Who would give this condition to our daughter? I could *never* believe in such a 'God'. And I never will!"

Needless to say, there was a shocked silence all around the dining room table. Fortunately, with a little pressure under the table by way of Mary's foot on mine, I said nothing. I can report that the couple stopped seeing us as friends from that night. They left our church, too.

This was wounding to me, and not a little humbling, but also instructive, I hope. I learned how easily the deep truth of the monism of God can be turned into something glib and uncompassionate. Inexplicable suffering and sorrow is bewildering for us all and can be deeply threatening to faith. The temptation to 'explain it away' is so strong. It is no wonder that the reaction can be so explosive. Pastorally speaking, appeal to the monism of God is an 'unstable compound'. Experience shows that it is as liable to detonate in your face as it is to help. 'Use at your own risk!' But this doesn't make it untrue.

Let me try to state as simply as I can the implications of Fr. Keating's Welcoming Prayer. It means that everything in your life proceeds from the mind and plan of God. Every reversal, every disappointment, every loss, every rejection and hurt of any kind, as well as every success, every fulfilled hope, every positive gain, every beloved acceptance and personal salve of any kind, is from the same Source.

I would say that for Boomers, i.e., the generation who are now entering or are already within the last third of our lives, the conviction that is expressed in the Welcoming Prayer is more likely to win resonance than it will from Millennials and those who are hard-slogging through the second third of life. It is easier for Boomers to agree with the Welcoming Prayer simply because the passage of time has borne it out. We have "seen with our eyes ... and our hands have handled" (I John 1:1) the resolution of early losses into later gains, the transformation of earlier defects and false starts into well shaded avenues and longer fulfillments. Therefore "Time Is On My Side" (Irma Thomas/Rolling Stones, 1964).

Both-And is also Either-Or

Yet I am still also a dualist, too.

I still see the hand of demonic opposition in much that is negative and malignant in the world and in my life.

While we pray the Welcoming Prayer every week at church, we also acknowledge, at the Pentecostal "Power Night" we visit Sunday nights, the heroic depth of St. Paul's Epistle to the Ephesians, where he writes, "We wrestle not against flesh and blood, but against principalities, against powers, against the rulers of the darkness of this world, against spiritual wickedness in high places" (6:12).

Funny this. The Welcoming Prayer covers it all. Yet we still also receive St. Paul's diagnosis that the world contains unseen enemies and malign antagonists. We gladly take part in a service where the Pentecostal pastor and her team rebuke and cast out maleficent intrusions from "the pit of hell." Then again, on the same night as the pastor is exorcizing demons in the Name of Jesus, we hear with heartfelt encouragement her comprehensive reflection that all, and she means all, griefs, burdens, and oppositions, ultimately derive from the same benign and divine Source.

This is what I meant when I said we are monists and dualists at the same time.

Gratitude in Place of Repulsion

That 'good outcome' to our life which we all desire in some form or another is characterized by peace and hope. The hope part I haven't gotten to yet—that's for the next chapter—but peace should be starting to flow like a river now. It is the peace which results from abreacted feeling and from the Hand of God, Who delivers us from suppressed, resistant evil threatening to stay attached to us even when we die. The un-released evil that has stayed with us, indissolubly attached, from the damaging deviations we made for ourselves in life—and which others also made for us—threatens to accompany us after death. "Someday lady, you'll accomp'ny me" (Bob Seger, 1980). Marley said it to Scrooge in *A Christmas Carol* as they looked out Scrooge's window and discerned multitudes of human souls scudding through the winter air, their legs attached to "the chains they wrought in life." You don't want that to happen to you.

Gratitude is a core constituent of peace.

Think of the experiences you have had and the influences you have suffered that could in no way have been interpreted at the time as helpful or warm. Think of the people who have rejected you and come against you with an ill will. There may not have been many such, but there have been a few. For myself, I can count 10 or 15 'wrong moves' I made that I regret deeply. I can certainly count 10 or 15 people of whom I got on the wrong side, or they of me. I can count only three or four individuals who have actively hated me and hatched plans of hostile intent. They are the most difficult. For their role in my life, gratitude seems completely counter-intuitive.

How, honestly, is one to ascribe any degree of goodness to those hostile persons, or even to the serious errors in judgment I made at any number of points along the way? Those were baleful choices and malicious people.

Yet do I wish to conclude my life with their gloating and unfeeling faces 'watching over me'? Or do I want to see the bright angels? Do I desire to go back and keep going back over certain ridiculous decisions, anchored in prideful fallacies about myself, that I made? And made again? Then made again?

Absolutely not.

What the Welcoming Prayer teaches, and what Joseph's insight in the Book of Genesis (50:20) establishes, is that every aspect of my life that repulses me has, in hindsight, turned out to have been for my good in the long run. And that is not just a papering over of the cracks in service of denial. It is a fact which is observable empirically.

Even the 'Southern Lady' of whom I spoke, who 'lost it' during the dinner party, may have changed her mind over the 20 years since that scene took place. You look at your worst fall from grace, your worst stumble, and your worst misfortune, and after 20 years there is almost always something, either within you or just outside, that developed out of it to the improvement of your life. Even if it was just a better empathy for other sufferers, or a better compassion for yourself in the face of the inner voice of criticism that has accompanied you since childhood. Or maybe it's been a development in the life of someone else you love, whose original misfortune and pain caused you your 'justified' anger at God.

The English poet William Cowper (d. 1800) said it famously and well:

> Ye fearful saints fresh courage take,
> The clouds ye so much dread
> Are big with mercy, and shall break
> In blessings on your head.
> Judge not the Lord by feeble sense,
> But trust him for his grace;
> Behind a frowning providence,
> He hides a smiling face.
> His purposes will ripen fast,
> Unfolding ev'ry hour;
> The bud may have a bitter taste,
> But sweet will be the flow'r.

Gratitude at the End of Life

There is nothing like, literally nothing like, a dying person who evinces seamless gratitude for his or her life. In all the deathbed vigils of which I have been a part, only five or six—though that sounds high as I write it down—attended a person who was explicitly grateful for his life as it had been lived. Almost all the other deathbed vigils were tainted with regret.

At a hospital in Charleston, South Carolina, I sat with a dying and rather ancient G.P. He was 'not a happy camper,' to say the least, and was explicitly regretful and pained, I would say, during his brief, daily moments of alertness. His wife, who loved him and sought to comfort him, kept going back to one patient in his long practice, a teenage girl whom he had saved from dying, and talking to him about her. She meant to convey the importance and essential goodness of his life as a doctor. But he could not hear it. Or rather, he would not hear it! It was like a drop of rain to put out a wildfire. This man died unhappy, resistant, and moderately bitter in relation to everything he had been and done.

At a hospital in Silver Spring, Maryland, a parishioner was at the end and most earnestly distressed in her mind. It proved too late to be able to hear whatever it was that was upsetting her. Something also unknown to her daughter, who was tirelessly by her mother's side, was causing this dying woman to be immensely upset. All that her daughter could finally do, and it did help but didn't do wonders, was to ask me to sing the hymn, "Jesus calls us o'er the tumult / Of our life's tempestuous sea." I had to sing it over and over in that hospital room, for it seemed to have some good effect. But consider those words: "the tumult / Of our life's tempestuous sea." This was the patient's life as she groaned and shuttled endlessly back and forth from side to side in her narrow, confining hospital bed.

I have one more illustration: my Mary's father lay dying in the hospital. He was attached to a ventilator for several days near the end. Mary was present when the technician finally received the order to take out the tube. There were days of pain and discomfort written all over her father's face when he was finally free of the large, intrusive device.

It would have been normal and fully human for her father at that moment to have said something like, "Finally! What took them so long. I am so relieved to be rid of that terrible thing. It was the worst!"

But that is not what Mary's father said. Right after the unhooking procedure, he looked gratefully at the technician and said simply, "Thank you, so much. That makes me feel much better. Thank you."

The 'attitude of gratitude' that Mary witnessed in her father was typical of him, and yet untypical of the hospital environment.

Extreme distress was all around—bed pans at best, intubation and catheters at worst: "Mona Lisas and Mad Hatters" (Elton John, 1972). Yet one patient evinced gratitude. One patient said thank you.

Not "The Worst That Could Happen"
(Johnny Maestro & Brooklyn Bridge, 1968)

Nothing happens without causation, or better, without an unseen plan. Even "The Worst That Could Happen" (Johnny Maestro & Brooklyn Bridge, 1968) has a corollary: don't take this present symptom, this dark besetting hour, at face value. There is more to it than you can see.

I don't expect anyone who is reading this to take my words to heart just because I say them. Rather, examine yourself. Boomers are fortunate on this line. By definition, Boomers have more years of elapsed experience through which to detect a 'backstory' that seems to fit their 'front-story.' God's "smiling face" (William Cowper) actually does come out from behind the curtain. The person who hurt you 'set you up' for the person who now loves you. A stab in the back pushed you into a zone which you would never have entered if it weren't for that sharp 'incentive.' The early loss of mother or father made you unusually open to love, real love, and also sensitive to it. Funny thing is, what I am writing actually occurs.

So take "The Worst That Could Happen" again, and look at it. You are old enough now, O bemused Boomer, to gaze on it with a touch of detachment. You have now felt the impacted pain of it, with the help of a good listener. You have also sought the Supernatural Power of God, and someone in touch with that Power prayed concretely for your deliverance. So look again at the worst thing that ever happened to you. It was and it became the thing of which you could say, with Hall & Oates, "You Make My Dreams" (1980). Just substitute the word "Nightmares" for "Dreams." It's got to go! You don't want a younger version of me singing verses from an old hymn into your ravaged ear and brain someday pretty soon, while your body turns fruitlessly over the bed pan at 60 RPM.

You want to hit the mark. So observe the monistic God at the root of that impacted nightmare.

Fake Nightmare

Did you ever see the original *Outer Limits* episode entitled "Nightmare"? It was broadcast in December 1963. It gave me an 'early warning system' to detect the benevolence that can exist behind apparent malevolence.

In "Nightmare" a group of Earth soldiers have been made prisoners-of-war by "Ebonites" from the Planet Ebon. The Earth soldiers are being tortured and harshly interrogated by cruel, implacable Ebonites, who want information from them. It turns out—and please don't object to 'spoilers' when they concern a 57-year-old TV show—that the whole thing is a fake. It is all a stage set, a piece of theater designed to test and evaluate the loyalty and resolution of Earth soldiers in the event of an inter-planetary war. The dreadful environment of Ebon has been artificially created to basically reward a unit of courageous, heroic earthmen.

I was 12 when I saw "Nightmare" and definitely never wanted to see it again. (Although my reason for hating it was not its "monism," but the fact that the Ebonite monsters turned out to be fake. I liked them real! They were only cool if they were real. Every 12-year-old boy at the time would have agreed.)

But the point, in fact, of the episode, and there have been many stories and movies like it, is that a bad thing turns out to be curative and good. The imposition of hell proves to be in the service of heaven.

The 12-year-old couldn't see that then. The 69-year-old roots for it now and is buoyed by it.

Gratitude is an emotion rooted in the observation that God's Grace is the energy within every given circumstance and opposition. In the long view there is nothing finally not to be grateful for. If you don't have gratitude, you will not die well. Your gratitude, or lack of it, is what will be remembered about the outcome of your life. ┼┼┼

CHAPTER FIVE

"Where I Am Going"

Where I am going there will be no compromise,
No tears will come to cloud my eyes,
Where I am going.
And all the precious world I've had to sacrifice
Will be given to me twice
Because He paid the price.
And it's worth it all just knowing
Where I am going.
Do you want to go riding with me
To a place that lasts forevermore?
Please don't think that you are one among the few.
I'm different just like you.

(Glen Campbell/Jimmy Webb, 1991)

While gratitude and peace are essential for a 'good death,' hope for some form of a personal future is also a necessary gift that makes it possible for a person to go, or rather, to let go. If I have no hope of a future 'state,' which is the old-fashioned word for it, then all I do have is either a resigned acceptance of complete nullification; or, which is probably worse, a question that carries no trace of an answer and can only produce the anxiety of an enigma. I am either 'going nowhere fast' or going somewhere but have no idea where. Does anyone really want to come to the end of life with either a certainty of extinction or a total uncertainty about "Where I Am Going"?

I think we can know something about the afterlife, and that is the subject of this chapter.

"Cast Your Fate to the Wind" (Vince Guaraldi, 1963)

In 2015 Lucas Hnath published a play entitled *The Christians*. It was performed at Playwrights Horizons in New York City, and my wife and I saw it.

The Christians concerns a white evangelical pastor who morphs into a theological liberal, thus disturbing his wife greatly and alienating his more conservative African-American associate pastor. Towards the end of the play, there is a scene in which the young associate pastor describes the death of his mother. I had never seen anything like this scene on a mainstream Manhattan stage, so I went out and bought the play. Here are the key lines:

> ASSOCIATE PASTOR
> And I said [to my mother],
> "Then just say you believe, say it with me, say
> 'I believe in Jesus, and I believe
> He died for my sins,' say it with me,"
> and she said,
> "I would like to say I believe,
> but if I did it would be a lie."
> I said,
> "But maybe that's enough—
> Say you believe in the hope that
> as you say you believe you will believe
> and maybe you'll truly believe."
> And she said,
> "Honey, I am going, I am leaving this earth,

and I will not spend my final breath
sayin' a damn lie,"
and she said, "When I close my eyes,
my eyes won't open again.
And when I close these eyes,
I'll see black,
and there will never again be
anything but."
...
But before her eyes closed and closed for good,
there was a moment,
a moment that was terror,
dread,
pain —
our eyes connected, and she saw me seeing her
fall,
and at that moment, her hand reached out
and grabbed my wrist, like she was grabbing for help.

I, for one, believe this scene. I believe it is true to life and true to the deathbed of physical life.

Partly I believe it because I have seen that look before, a look of transfixed terror at the moment of death or right before it. Once I was with a man at the very point of death and was the only other person in the room. On his face I saw that exact look of terror as he expired. He was falling somewhere, and I could do nothing to catch him.

I also believe the scene from *The Christians* because I fear death myself and am sometimes in touch, personally, with the play character's terror of an immense fall, like the poor sailors whom King Kong shakes off an ancient tree in the 1933 movie, who flail at the air and scream as they fall to the rocks 100 feet below.

We all die whether we like it or not, and we all die whether our vital question is answered or not concerning "Where I Am Going." In other words, we all die whether we are agnostic about the future, hopeless about it, or hopeful about it. But there is a measureless distance between having hope at the point of death and having no hope.

What are our grounds for hope at the point of death?

The state of death is, almost needless to say, an "undiscover'd country from whose bourne / no traveler returns" (*Hamlet*, Act III, Scene I). What empirical facts or observations are there to create a case for survival of the human person after his or her body ceases to live? Is it possible, on the basis of observable evidence, to have some idea about the state of a person after they die? Is there anything we can know? That is the subject of this chapter: our grounds for a sustaining hope in a future life at the approach of physical death.

Memory

I wrote earlier about the persisting objects of memory. In particular, I mentioned the unquenchable memories of a person's early connection to love, memories that seem never to fade. I mentioned a friend who persistently rebuffs my mentioning unhappy experiences we shared in college by saying almost dismissively, "That happened so long ago." I observed that the longer it was *ago*, the more likely it is to have stayed with you.

To put it another way, if something important happened to you in the first third of your life, and especially in the childhood phase of that first third, it usually has a longer 'shelf life' than if it took place later. The further away the event is in time, the closer to you is the memory. I gave the illustration of my parishioner whose Alzheimer's put him forever before the draft board in 1917, where he had told a lie, the painful recollection of which was literally all he was able to talk about right through to the mid-1980s when I used to visit him in the nursing home. He is long dead but may still be sitting before that draft board somewhere. I think he probably took the decisive, excruciating incident with him when he died.

What is it that does not fade or get lost in your mental recollections? So much does get lost. I can barely remember the names of the church wardens and vestry in our last parish 11 years ago. But I can give you the first, middle, and last names of almost every member of my college fraternity, not to mention the affectionate nicknames we had for each one of them.

Your early relationships rarely if ever 'leave the building.' This tells you that childhood and adolescent connections tap something very deep. The core urge to connect with another soul is primary in life. It must be inbuilt for it to be so powerful and prevalent. If any element of the human makeup is indestructible, it is the urge to *bridge* to another. In the case of everyone reading this book, I hope it worked!

What makes the aging process of Charles Foster Kane in *Citizen Kane* so affecting and also wrenching, is the man's unconscious hold on, or rather, his being held by, the memory of his mother's loss to him at age 8. In the last third of his life, which begins when his second wife leaves him, Citizen Kane has only the memory of his lost primal maternal love to sustain him. And so he dies in complete consternation, but yet speaking a name, "Rosebud," which is what he called the ancient childhood sled that is the sole material object he still possesses from his "Lost Lenore."

I think you can say that Charles Foster Kane goes to his death, his "soul takes flight" (Plato's *Phaedo*), carrying one possession—the early connection he had with his mother. He dies the way many people die, if they are conscious at all—bereft and reaching out.

We had a World War II hero in our parish once, a man who had gone down with a cruiser that was torpedoed by the Japanese. I believe it was during the Battle of Leyte Gulf. He survived, but barely. He told me that he and about three hundred of his fellow sailors were able to get off the cruiser just before it sank but not in time to reach the lifeboats. As these helpless men, most of them in their early 20s or even younger, were bobbing in the oil-slicked, fiery water, many of them cried out for their mothers. Not their wives—few of them had one—nor another 'bracket' of persons, but their mothers. It was the strongest memory that this good man had of that unforgettable moment. Many of his shipmates died near him in the water with their mother's name on their lips. Do you remember the most popular song on the Union side during the Civil War? It was called "Just Before the Battle, Mother (I Was Thinking Most of You)."

This is not to reduce the lasting part of a person to his or her relationship to their mother. But it is a clue to the feeling which is most important, and basically unsubduable, in human nature and in individual beings: the memory of an historic and unrepeatable intimate personal connection. It is one thing you never lose—the memory, I mean. And if you never had it, or it got ruptured, you never lose *that* memory, either.

"Soul-Ties"

I am searching here for some evidence of the survival of the soul after death. I am looking for elements in the life cycle of everyday people that might be identified as unquenchable, inexhaustible, or better yet, indestructible. Let's say we are looking for "The Unsinkable Molly Brown" of a human being.

I use the word "soul" because it is what we are talking about. It is evident empirically that the body does not survive its own death. There is no feeling or consciousness left in the body after it has died. The body may take a while to actually and definitively die, i.e., to be in the state according to which the coroner can sign its death certificate. All signs of physical life have to cease in order for the doctor to pronounce the body dead. And we dispose of the body, within varying customs and preferences, as an object that has no feeling and no consciousness. Patients facing death sometimes say of their funerals, "Well, *I* won't be there! So you people can do anything you wish." Other people, usually those in good health, deliver specific and detailed instructions—rarely followed in full, by the way, by their nearest and dearest—for their funeral. Whether *laissez-faire* or precisely requested, the governing thought is that the dying person will not be there, in the flesh, to dictate terms.

But the unseen part of the person, the percipient part you cannot see, is the soul, or spirit. It was in the body during the person's life, but it is not there when they are dead.

I have tried for many years to understand the distinction that different traditions within Christianity try to make between the "soul" and the "spirit." The distinction always seems to be a form of words. Try it yourself. Try to identify the difference between soul and spirit. I think you will end up diving into a deep well of abstraction. All you need to know here, in this book, in order to start imagining "Where I Am Going," is that there is an incorporeal element within every person that is his or her essential consciousness and subjective personal being.

This incorporeal element, the soul, is focused, at its deepest urge, on linking with the incorporeal element of another human being. That is evident from the way memory works, and I have been 'culling' that observation about memory during almost 50 years of pastoral ministry.

"Yikes, Terri!"

We were attending a Pentecostal conference in 2018 where one of the speakers was Terri Savelle Foy. I had never heard of this speaker, though everyone else there seemed to have. Her outward presentation and 'style,' by which I mean both her appearance and the way she delivered her message, were unfamiliar. It seemed to this traditionally minded Episcopalian like a combination of *Seventeen* magazine and a chatty form of Christian fundamentalism. To tell you the truth, I almost switched her off at first because of the externals.

But I was wrong. Terri Savelle Foy caught my attention about a third of the way into her talk when she spoke about something she called "soul-ties." It turned out this phrase was familiar within Pentecostal circles, though, again, I had never heard it. Chalk that up to having lived too long in a mainline ecclesiastical ghetto.

"Soul-ties" were a big gap in my preparation. They were not a gap in my *life*, for I knew about them in practice. But I had never given them a name, at least not in theological language. The term "soul-tie" shed light on a phenomenon I had experienced in life and also observed in others, as well as in literature. The term also began to shed light on the subject of life's continuance after death.

Terri Savelle Foy taught us during her talk that intimate

physical relationships create a bond or "tie" between two people that can turn obdurate and almost impossible to break later on. That is to say, when the bond or tie of a close physical relationship gets broken situationally for good and explicable reasons—such as when you break up or get divorced because of abuse or unfaithfulness or just towering changes in life goals and aspirations—there may still exist between you a "soul-tie," which only God can break. You are separated physically and geographically from the person you once loved, but your souls are still connected. Invisible wires! In the case of a soul-tie, you can run but you cannot hide.

Part of this teaching comes from St. Paul, who observed in I Corinthians 6:16 that when a person joins his or her body to another person in sex, they become a part of you, almost organically. A "soul-tie" is the "tie that binds" a lover to his or her object (of past or present love), and it can be so tight—remember the song "Tighter, Tighter" by Alive N Kickin (1970)?—that you cannot untie it. It is too tight and too complexly tied for you to untie it yourself. It can tie *you* up, however, in a big huge knot, forever and ever.

When Terri Savelle Foy's talk opened up within me—her somewhat bemused-at-first listener—a kind of Pandora's Box of self-understanding, the Holy Spirit struck! For that reason, she is forever within my catalogue of earthly angelic helpers. I learned from her as follows:

First, I had had a couple of soul-ties. One had proved exceptionally hard to break. The tie *had* been broken, through the direct ministration of another Pentecostal preacher. But I had never understood why it had been so resilient in a negative sense. Terri Savelle Foy opened that up. She declared that of all the talks she had ever given, her talk on "soul-ties" had proven the most popular—by far! Countless viewers and hearers of it had said that her talk on soul-ties was the most helpful thing she had ever done for them. I was now in that queue. The term shed light on something that had bothered me for many years.

Second, the phrase "soul-tie" opened a new window into my thinking about eternal life. What, empirically I mean, endured when all else lapsed? In experience, that is, what aspects of one's inward life seemed so strong that even when everything else faded, such as strength of body and eyesight and hearing, or 'all of the above,' even then some element or elements survived? Soul-ties were obviously one of them. And maybe the most potent of all.

Those drowning, burning sailors who were crying so pitiably to their mothers as their torpedoed ship sank. The dying persons I had attended who were focussed on ancient, and I mean *ancient*, pain from lost or separated relationships. That desperate woman in the Silver Spring hospital, groaning for someone or something and moving constantly in her bed, reaching out for a handle she couldn't find. And many other incomplete lives and people with whom I had been present at or near the point of death.

This included my own mother, whose dying hours were spent on the floor of a downstairs half-bathroom, repelling the very people on the other side of the door who were trying hard to help her.

The outcome of many people's lives is not a good one. "Somethin' inside has died" (Carole King, 1971)—long ago—but its 'funeral,' what we today like to call 'closure,' never took place. Somewhere inside the person is a soul-tie, and to break it you need—guess what—the Supernatural Power of God.

Past loss, past rejection, and past hurt in relation to unbreakable soul-ties do not die without 'heap big medicine.' As I watched all these good people in my parishes trying to unbind themselves, I realized I was being given a clue to the part of us which is eternal. You could almost say that my first empirically verifiable evidence of personal eternity was the Gordian Knot of the "soul-tie."

"Drink to Me Only with Thine Eyes"

The soul-tie that is the essence of romantic love is not only something in itself—stubborn and resistant in its hold on you—but it points towards a penetrating, universal phenomenon of human existence. From birth we are focussed on immediate one-to-one connection. Every haunting decision of our emotional life derives from the need either to make that connection or compensate for its disruption.

Hear these quintessential Motown lyrics by the Four Tops from 1964:

> Without the one you love, life is not worthwhile.
> Without your love, my dear, I'm like a fatherless child.
> So come and fill my empty arms and
> Make my life worthwhile.
> Sometimes I feel like a wanderer
> (Got to have your love right now)
> Searching for peace within
> (Baby I need your good lovin')
> I need you, my darling
> Like a lost soul needs a friend.

This all-animating motive, deriving from the most original source within the human being, endures right through to the point of death, its very brink, when all you want is someone to hold your hand.

Remember King Henry VIII, who got almost everything he wanted during the second third of his life. At the moment of his death, however, all he wanted was to hold his Archbishop Thomas Cranmer's firm right hand.

"We went together for so long / Every second record on the radio seemed like our song" (Burton Cummings, 1997)

Here is an impression that is undeniable from experience—and from Top 40 listings—but people don't always want to hear it. I often get pushback when I talk about the urge for connection, most typically romantic connection, as being the most powerful human drive.

But hey, why do you like the music you like? More specifically, if you're a Boomer, *why do you like the music you like?* I will bet you—if you're a Boomer, that is—that the music to which you are drawn, like the "tractor beam" in *Star Wars,* is the music you listened to when you were in high school or college. I'll bet you a second time that your 'mother lode' of cherished tunes derives from times when you were in love.

Look, just go on the comments section for almost any album or single track that's available on iTunes. For that matter, scan the comments section of any YouTube upload of a song you remember. About 90% of the comments go something like this: "I first heard this tune when I was 15 and I can't get it out of my head. It reminds me of …" Or, "My mom used to have this album on the record player when my sister and I would get home from school. It makes me remember those wonderful times we had together." Or, "I can't hear that song without thinking of my first boyfriend. We didn't make it and I don't even know what happened to him. But this song, OMG."

Try the exercise yourself. Go on iTunes and scan the comments on the oldies but goodies. (Scan your *own*, not-yet-printed comments.)

What is being said in the vast majority of these responses is that the song itself is not the point. The artistry, the performers, the writer, the historical context: these are not the point. They may be interesting, but they are not the point. The point is *when* you heard the song, *how* you heard it, and with *whom* you heard it. The point, in other words, is you!

Wait a minute, goes the objection! You mean that this is really *not* about wailing Robert Plant and "Immigrant Song"? It's not about cool Brian Ferry and "Virginia Plain"? It's not about E. L. O.?—and Van Halen—and Billy Idol—and Deborah Harry? It's not about the Grateful Dead and Janice Ian and the Tams?

No. It's not about any of them. *It's about you.*

In fact, just about every novel, movie, and song you have ever loved is about one thing: where you were—who you were—in heart, body and mind—when you encountered it.

Who is the 'You' We are Talking About?

The Catholic spiritual writer Thomas Keating made a big impression on contemporary religious thought with his distinction between what he called the "true self" and the "false self." It was Thomas Merton who in our time first wrote about that distinction. It is a fairly ancient distinction in Christian mysticism, but Fr. Keating, following on Thomas Merton, was its chief popularizer and exponent.

Fr. Keating saw the human being as an amalgam of two "personalities" or self-understandings. These two "selves" are to some extent in conflict.

A person's "true self" is the part of them that is connected to God, the part of them that is divine in substance, origin, and destination. It is the *imago dei* in each of us (Genesis 1:26), the soul.

A person's "false self" is the part of them that is his or her individual subjectivity, the entity inside you that is ego, superego, and id all rolled into one. The "false self" is what Scripture calls the "natural man" (I Corinthians 2:14), the "old man" (Romans 6:6; Ephesians 4:22; Colossians 3:9), and the "carnal mind" (Romans 8:7).

So there is PZ, my immortal soul created in the image of God, who was born looking for his direct link with God—restoring what was broken at birth—and whose true self is animated by the need and desire to be one with God, with uniting Love, really. This true self is the motive force behind every emotional decision I have ever made. For me it is the beginning, the end, what existed before the beginning, and what will exist after the end. The true self is eternal.

Meanwhile, though, there is PZ's false self, a tremulous, eyes-in-the-back-of-his-head, anxious sort of person. He is fearful and worried and subject to never-ending stress. This PZ is concerned passionately with honor, money, and control; and is, if his false self voice were really able to come through and be heard loud and clear upon the surface of his life, a self-damning and pretty alienating character.

The trouble is, and the central issue of life is, that the true self lives on after we die, while the false self stays behind—somewhere, but not with God, for God is "of purer eyes than to behold evil" (Habakkuk 1:13). The true self is what we usually call the soul. The false self is what gets buried, with perhaps a nod, if you're lucky, on the deceased person's headstone.

A Descent into Empathy

This little handbook for Boomers is much more concerned about your true self than your false one. The true self is the part of you of which St. Paul says, "Behold, we live!" (II Corinthians 6:9). Your true self, and its extension by means of the connection that is forged with another's true self, i.e., one-to-one love, is the sole thing that really matters in life. Or rather, everything that matters in your life—the persons and experiences you will have on your mind as you prepare to die (if they haven't over-medicated you, which is likely)—derives from the inborn and thus entirely legitimate drive to connect with another and exist in union rather than separation.

When I say that everyone has a "true self," I mean it. It covers everyone.

This should be able to help us with compassion, let alone tolerance, for even the most distorted or twisted person in the world has a true self. Everyone in the world has a reason for what they do. It is usually connected with a search for connection, or the wounding that was caused by a disruption of that connection. Find the way into a person's true self, or what remains of it, and you probably have them forever.

Francis Dolarhyde

The creator of the television show *Miami Vice*, Michael Mann, directed an intense, memorable, and radical movie concerning this theme. The movie is called *Manhunter* (1986) and stars William Petersen, Tom Noonan, and Kim Greist. Petersen plays a detective who is searching for a psychotic serial killer before the killer commits his next horrible crime. The perpetrator is extremely shrewd. The man's name turns out to be Francis Dolarhyde.

Manhunter hones in on the detective's near-compulsion to get inside the mind of his target. It takes him a lot of deep breaths, natural disgust, and gifted courage to do his work. He and we find out that Francis Dolarhyde's true self exists in relation to a misbegotten desire for union with a mythological creature out of the poetry of William Blake. Dolarhyde also sincerely loves a blind young woman, who is able, unknowingly, to restrain for a time his murderous psyche. All this about Francis Dolarhyde is shown, though not so much as to make him sympathetic as to make him plausible. The hero does get his man. No one who has seen *Manhunter* will ever be able to listen to "In-A-Gadda-Da-Vida" again.

I use these illustrations to demonstrate the fact that everyone has a true self, albeit in perpetual 'conversation,' or more likely, conflict, with his nervous ego self. Your true self is inevitably and *toujours* "Looking for a love to call my own" (J. Geils Band, 1971).

"Nervous Man in a Four Dollar Room" (1960)

We want a good outcome to our lives. We didn't think about it too much when we were barreling through the second third of our lives. (The false self took over during that second third.) But now it is on our mind.

Rod Serling wrote a half-hour teleplay for the original *Twilight Zone* in 1960 and it was produced as the episode entitled "Nervous Man in a Four Dollar Room." Wish I could show the episode to everyone who has ever lived. It encapsulates the decisive point of transformation in a person's life, the pivot-point from one's false self to one's true self, in a completely believable yet wonderfully brief situation.

Joe Mantell plays Jackie Rhoades, a small-time thief waiting in a squalid hotel room for a call from George, who will give Jackie his next job. As he waits for George's call, Jackie looks in the mirror and, to his surprise, sees himself looking back to him. The Jackie who lives in the mirror berates the nail-biting, underling Jackie who sits anxiously in the hotel room. Hotel Jackie defends his life in the face of Mirror Jackie's criticism. Everything that comes out of the mouth of Mirror Jackie is true. Everything that comes out of Hotel Jackie is self-justifying and pathetic. Mirror Jackie is his true self; Hotel Jackie, his false self.

Finally, Hotel Jackie breaks the mirror and shuts down the threatening conversation from his end. At that moment, George, Jackie's criminal 'handler,' enters the room and vilifies Hotel Jackie for failing to do the assigned job, which was to murder a man.

It is then that the switch takes place.

When Hotel Jackie finally speaks up for himself in the face of George's threats, the viewer instantly sees that Mirror Jackie has come back. Conscientious Mirror Jackie has taken over, and servile Hotel Jackie is gone. At this point and in short order, Mirror Jackie expels George, leaves the pathetic hotel room forever, and announces that he will get a job, and maybe get married! Jackie's true self has won; his false self is banished.

If only this brilliant exchange could take place in everyone's life. Or at least before the stakes seem to have gotten lower because "the busy world is hushed, and the fever of life is over, and our work is done" (Cardinal Newman's Prayer). I wish with a whole heart that I had seen the truth of "Nervous Man in a Four Dollar Room" long before I did. Maybe I couldn't have heard it during the second third of life. But still I wish I had.

Now I'm a Boomer, and you are, too. Watch this episode of Rod Serling's original *Twilight Zone* and make it your own. If you don't, you will probably come to the end of the last third of your life no wiser nor more hopeful than you were at the end of the second third.

Holding onto Your False Self—for Dear Life!

Early on in our ministry we came face to face with an example of someone in the last third of his life who was holding on to his false self in a way that could have come straight out of Dickens or Thackeray.

This was a near-legendary attorney in Washington, D.C., who had had what the world calls a distinguished public career. He had not only made a great deal of money for himself and his family, but also had 'given back' a lot, both in public service and in philanthropic gifts to charities and educational institutions. (As I write that, I am lapsing into *New York Times* obituary-ese.) The man had also served on innumerable boards, most of them 'high-profile.' Even after his formal retirement from the practice of law, his name was still all over the place.

Mary and I knew him during the last third of his life. We kept getting invited to dinners and ceremonies at which he was the honored guest. He collected many—it seemed like about 200-plus—prizes and certificates, the most impressive of which were medals struck in his honor that had his face on them. These medals with his face on them were his proudest possession.

What we remember now was that he never seemed to stop wanting more medals to be cast in his honor. Nothing pleased him more than this: being awarded a medal from an overseas government or domestic foundation *that had his face on it*. His delight in being recognized by means of a large bronze coin or paperweight with his face on it never diminished. And we knew him even when he was a very old man. We also realized pretty quickly that the only way to be sure you had earned his good graces was if he gave you one of those medals. That was the sure sign of his favor.

When the distinguished man died—and we attended his gorgeous Episcopal funeral—we came to the end of our painful wait to receive a medal with his face on it. A friend of ours had received one shortly before the man died, and we comforted ourselves with the thought that if he had just lived a little longer, he would have 'awarded' one of them to us, too.

My point is that it is fully possible *never* to get detached, even to the smallest degree, from your false self. Our Washington friend, sagacious, mildly self-deprecating, always perfectly turned out and with the right thing to say, entirely in the political and cosmopolitan moment, was really after one thing. Or rather, there was one thing he loved above all others. I have told you what it was. I do not think he ever changed. And as I say, the many medals struck in his honor with his face on them are in a drawer somewhere, or in closed drawers within the houses of the few elect ones to which he had awarded one.

The Genius and the Goddess (1955)

What happens to your false self when you die? The true self, weak as its 'public' voice and hope may have been right up to the end, survives. We'll get to that. But what happens to PZ in the ego sense? What happens to him?

Here is how Aldous Huxley describes what happens, in his 1955 novel *The Genius and the Goddess*. The "Genius" of the title, Henry, is an impossibly self-absorbed human being, though a world-class scientist. His self-preoccupied life has not had a good outcome! At the end of the book Henry dies. The narrator of the novel is then asked by another character, What happened to Henry? Where is he now? Here is what the narrator says:

> God knows. Into some kind of infantile burrow in his subconscious, I suppose. Outside, for all to see and hear, was that stupendous clockwork monkey, that undiminished blaze of intellectual power. Inside there lurked the miserable little creature who still needed flattery and reassurance and sex and a womb-substitute—the creature who would have to face the music on Henry's deathbed. *That* was still frantically alive and unprepared by any preliminary dying, totally unprepared for the decisive moment. Well, the decisive moment is over now and whatever remains of poor old Henry is probably squeaking and gibbering in the streets of Los Alamos, or maybe around the bed of his widow and her new husband. And of course nobody pays any attention, nobody gives a damn. Quite rightly. Let the dead bury their dead.

What a way to go.

The Code that Unlocks Your Life—in Hindsight

St. Paul compares a believer's faith, hope, and love in I Corinthians

13. He asks himself, which of these three great headlights with which a Christian navigates their way through life is the brightest and the best? Which of the three is the most important? And on what basis could we say that any one of them is more important than the other two? Turns out there *is* a basis for prioritizing one of them over the other two, and Paul does that.

The Apostle partially deconstructs faith and hope because neither of them, as positions or outlooks on life, survives after death. This is because faith, for the Christian when he or she dies, is fulfilled or realized. Faith is fulfilled at that point because the Object of faith, God in His Son Jesus Christ, is met in Person and thus 'gained' at that moment. You no longer need faith after you die because what was unseen but believed during your human life is now, according to St. Paul, actually seen. That in which you had faith during the time when you could not see it with your eyes, is now right in front of them.

Similarly, hope is superannuated at the point of death and beyond for the Christian, because the Object of hope, your future and eternal life with God in Christ, has been gained. What you had hoped for is no longer an unseen desire, but is now plainly in view— that is, for the Christian soul in the heaven of God. Hope is no longer required when its Object has come to you in Person.

Whether the reader believes any of this does not take away from the Biblical point in service of which faith and hope have fallen away like crutches that are no longer necessary for a person whose body is cured. For St. Paul, love, which is the nature and substance of the eternal connection between the believer and God, survives death. It is the "consummation devoutly to be wished." The one-to-one "soul-tie" that was aspired to with every ounce of one's strength in life, is now the ultimate chain and tie of which it was a subset. In quality the best soul-tie in life is one in nature with the eternal soul-tie that is unbreakable. More than that, the star to which your true self was unendingly looking to tie its wagon, when it was seeking that human connection, was actually God, is God, and will always henceforth be God.

Here is the code which makes the whole of your life plausible. It unlocks what is normally the mystery of a thousand false starts and almosts/could-have-beens. The true self, when it came out of the gate, which was your birthday, came out looking to renew its previous unbroken connection with God. When your soul arrived, in other words, it departed God. But it experienced 'buyer's remorse' from the moment it opened its eyes.

A whole nest of harpies, known in aggregate as the false self, descended on the newborn child and began their work. Traditional Christian theology says that you were born in sin. In other words, the minute your soul 'touched the ground,' the inherent givens of this world, the flesh, and the devil invaded your blood stream and made you into a fearful, hoarding, grasping, controlling entity. Your soul, the image of God within you, always knew better, deep down, but you weren't able to feel sure. On the one hand, your true self was focussed with devotion on the longed-for necessary one-to-one. But when that was disrupted, mainly by just growing up, you got confused by colored lights and multiple voices. You thought you could re-create your initial bliss by means of any number of possible connections, almost all of which were secondary, though you didn't know that at first. You didn't know it, in other words, until they crumbled down upon you and left your life in ruins.

The second third of life, your grown-up adult years, were spent mostly in pursuing false lead after false lead, false step after false track after false glimpse. O Boomer, fill in the blanks. You were chronically in search of an object to satisfy the grasping, needy, despairing part of you. But you always also remembered something important and seemingly non-repeatable: the earliest oneness. The only place where that seemed to be approximated was the connection you had with the person or persons with whom you fell in love. And it was approximated there! When your eyes would meet, something befell you. "The eyes have it!" When I first met my Mary, it was her eyes (and her smile) that had me, right then and there.

The day you met her, you were back at day one, year one, phase one. Nothing succeeded like romantic love in awakening the unique remembered feeling of intimate connection. It was a feeling, remember, that preceded even your birthday. It was the way it was with you and God before He pushed you out into this world. (Don't ask me why He did that, but He did.)

So now you have gotten to retirement age. While you've had some close calls with true love, maybe one, maybe two, at most three, things have gotten obscured by a great many 'bunny trails.' Money didn't do it for you. Status didn't do it. Control did it a little, but you're not quite as sharp and 'on it' as you were. You can't help falling behind a little now. So if you are wise, the consuming interests of the second third of your life have faded in force. Unfortunately, those interests are still trying to con you. They are certainly conning an old college friend of mine who just *has* to be catered to as someone important when she travels, even if it means she has to give away all her money to an institution so *they* will fly her there (in order, actually, to cajole more funds out of her). False promises from the second third of life can surely haunt you during the last third. They can, in fact, preoccupy you then. But death can come suddenly, too, and you are unprepared.

Boomer, get prepared! At one stunning, unrepeatable moment, which often comes by surprise, the dedications of your second third of life will prove sterile and unhelpful. They will evanesce, leaving only a bewildered, shocked you in the moment following your death, in the presence of the Light that is the Light of Men.

Forgiving You Your False Self

Let's say you are tracking with me. For the sake of argument, let's agree that this picture of a false and a true self 'vying' for survival and significance is basically accurate, or at least true to life. No typology is ever completely accurate, but let's just say this one covers the main aspiration and the main disappointments of an everyday life.

If the true self is the God part of us, the soul that God Himself implanted in this body, His image (Genesis 1:26) that lives there; and if the true self is therefore going back to God at the point of death, even having had some experience of the God-relation within this mortal coil, then what happens to the false self? What happens at death to the 'Paul Zahl' part of me, which believed so much of the nonsense of what "flesh is heir to"? What happens to my thousands of memories, associations, concepts, opinions, interests, projections, dreams in sleep, confusions, misunderstandings, falsehoods, phases, you name it? What happens to my false self and its many constituent elements? Is it enough for the *true* self, as "the soul takes flight," to simply say *sayonara* to that narrow-minded false self that remains behind "squeaking and gibbering," which is Huxley's phrase? Is the picture that of a helicopter lifting off the ground with the true self as passenger, who all he or she can do is wave a little wistfully at the devastated, disappointed, left-behind turd on the ground; and then the whirlybird disappears forever?

Behold: **Here is where the Christian Gospel has a unique and overwhelmingly existential contribution to make to any account of the tragic human story.** Here is where the Gospel that Mockingbird, in particular, expresses most aptly in our time and was founded to teach, delivers an impact so riveting and delivering that it alters the entire pathetic scene.

"As Far as the East is From the West" (Psalm 103:12): The Great Divorce

Here we go
Climbing the stairway to heaven
Here we go
Walking the road of ecstasy
Taking the load
Of this whole world off our shoulders
The door is wide open for you
The door open for me
You and I
We are gonna find the pirates' treasure
Talkin' 'bout heaven right here on earth
Gonna make it real, gonna make it real

In their Philadelphia Soul classic from 1975, entitled "Stairway to Heaven," The O'Jays are feeling close to God. Close to God, that is, to the extent that the singer and his lover share the unitive ecstasy that is their closest thing on earth to heaven. The song—and just about every other popular song that has ever been a Top-40 hit—evokes in pure form the soul-tie link that feels like the nearest thing in life to eternal bliss.

But because it is to a person, because the soul-tie is to a human being, it is not enough. The true self, as distinct from the false self, is only satisfied with the ultimate soul-tie, mediated, yes, through another's eyes, but ultimately beyond any human being. The true self has already climbed the "stairway to heaven." Or better, when it was born into a human body, the true self descended the stairway from heaven. For a time the true self left its heavenly home with God. For the true self now, heaven is an instance of recognition.

Love of another human being is the true self's great "Intimation of Immortality" (Wordsworth, 1807). But the false self is struggling behind, on foot, dragging a huge, bulky chest of false starts and inadequate, disappointed possibilities, let alone crimes and misdemeanors.

What happens at death to the poor, out-of-breath false self? Or is he or she just left cold by that rapidly rising helicopter that has already half disappeared behind the clouds?

"This is a True Saying, and Worthy of All to be Received, that Christ Jesus Came into the World to Save Sinners" (I Timothy 1:15)

St. Bartholomew is often portrayed in art as carrying his own skin. That is because he was martyred by being flayed alive. There is another figure, Marsyas in Greek mythology, who was skinned alive for angering Apollo by competing with him—'successfully'—in a musicians' contest. As punishment for his hubris, Marsyas was flayed by Apollo and his skin tied to a tree.

In Charles Dickens's *A Christmas Carol*, the dead who don't end well, the dead whose lives fail to achieve the good outcome this book is talking about, flitter through the skies. But they are *not* free as a bird. That is because those dead are tied to "the chains they wrought in life," from which they cannot unbind themselves. I believe this is a true picture of your impending future, O Boomer, if you do not begin to get this right.

What the Christian Word declares—the right verb for it—is the forgiveness of sins.

"God," as the Gospel chorus goes, "is a good God, yes, He is!" You don't have to enter His heaven still chained to your past. In fact, you can't enter Heaven if you are still chained to your past. Your skin, your false self, will not be tied to a tree for all to see. It sounds unashamedly simple, but it is the heart of the matter:

God wants to forgive you your false self.

Picture yourself a little like St. Bartholomew. The Renaissance sculptures of the saint are evocative. Bartholomew is in good shape physically, partly because he is now all taut muscle and clean bone. He is also carrying his *skin* in his hands, and over his shoulder. It is kind of billowing. "Accidentally like a martyr" (Warren Zevon, 1978), Bartholomew seems almost proud of his creased, detached, grisly gift.

This is a picture of how we can think of God's forgiveness pronounced in relation to our false selves. Remember Rod Serling's closing narration for the episode entitled 'Static'. We watched a man whose false self had shut him up into a state of embittered isolation and loneliness. Yet God stepped in. Serling concluded the story with these words: "Around and around she goes, and where she stops nobody knows. All Ed Lindsay knows is that he desperately wanted a second chance and he finally got it... in the Twilight Zone."

You were born a soul into a body. You were looking for love, the love from which you had been so rudely interrupted. But your embodied soul, once in the world, became a magnet for diverse and hostile pleadings. It became a kind of punching bag for false seductive possibilities and 'come-hithers.' "Come over here, and I will refresh you." "*I've* got what you are looking for." "Vanity Fayre, Vanity Fayre, come one, come all, all is vanity."

But by the end of the second third of your life, you were fairly exhausted. The exhaustion that overcame you was primarily inward, caused by the disappointment arising from many years of "looking for love in all the wrong places" (Johnny Lee, 1980).

Think of yourself at death a little like St. Bartholomew. Maybe you're ashamed a little—or a lot—by the sheer size of the thing, your false self. The skin you carry looks like Jabba the Hutt's. It's Yuge!

But size doesn't matter in relation to God. Whether the skin of your false self—your misconceived life's 'journey' with its many missteps—is diaphanous and fine, or whether it is thick, coarse, and tattooed, the quantity is not the essential fact about it. It covered you, that's all. It was the outward you, what you took pains to present and express. It bore, as you knew all along and as your daydreams kept informing you, little resemblance to your real and utterly sincere interest deep down, which ... was ... to find ... intimate one-on-one connection with one person. And he or she was always the surrogate for the One Person Whom you were looking for and Whom you really missed.

You probably aren't desiring to present your skin, as St. Bartholomew was entitled to do, with any sort of pride. No, it is "Kind of a Drag" (The Buckinghams, 1967). Off with it! To hell with it. Away with it.

This is our universal *viaticum*, God's forgiveness of our sin, for that temporary but engrossing 'state' which is our false self. The Christian *viaticum* applies to everyone potentially.

Everyone has a false self, and every true self is required to jettison the false one at the point of death. For some, they were prepared. Some were confessed and absolved before they died. Some were given to tell the truth about themselves before they died. Some saw through their compelled life before they had to.

Others, however, died with the skin attached tightly to every square inch of their soul's human incarnation. They never got flayed. And even if they did get flayed—by life!—they didn't want to know. They still *acted*, like our friend in love with the bronze medals of himself, as if they were the same thing as their false identity. They couldn't see the distinction—even though everyone else could, looking at them.

"Reflections of My Life"
(Marmalade, 1970)

If this sounds to some readers a little like 'gnosticism' or 'Platonic dualism,' it is not. It is simply the recognition—the observation, really—that people have two conflicting 'sides of the same coin' within them: the "natural man," i.e., the false self, of which St. Paul speaks; and the "new being," i.e., the true self, of which St. Paul also speaks. Each side of a person struggles for mastery. In practice the natural man wins most of the time. But the true self has its eyes ever open for the great Link, the Link which is more precious than anything else in the world and which people, real existential people, are willing to do anything, absolutely anything, to find and establish.

"When the Whip Comes Down"
(Rolling Stones, 1978)

O Boomer, your boom is coming down! I see it. It is like the jerry-rigged guillotine in *Horrors of the Black Museum* (1959), which a madman has constructed over your bed; and when you look up from your pillow, it is too late because the blade is already coming down. Get a hold of yourself before it is too late. "Repent, for the kingdom of heaven is at hand!" (Matthew 4:17). Just one word of repentance, one word of plain dealing, and it's gone. That's the way God is.

This is the one imperative at the root of this handbook for Boomers: "Stop and Get a Hold of Yourself" (Blue Magic, 1975). Drop your false self. Disillusion yourself, radically, of the phony, unfruitful concepts you had in your 30s, 40s, and 50s. "Lift up thine eyes." (Isaiah 60:4). Look up, look north. If you don't, I predict you will end up like the young pastor's defiant mother in *The Christians*, hurtling down a pitch-black well, alone and probably screaming.

Soul Survivors

A concluding word on "Where I Am Going": What is the final state of the true self, whose false self has been dropped and left behind by virtue of God's forgiveness of it? It has received 'closure,' and you won't have to give it another thought. It is no longer part of you. As the song says, you have said "goodbye to all the pain I used to know. / It's time to let it go."

But where are you going? You have made the journey, but it is not the destination. What will Heaven be like? Can we know anything specific or descriptive about it?

Johnson Over Jordan (1939)

I think the 20th-century British playwright J. B. Priestley (d. 1984) can help us.

Here are some of the last lines from Priestley's 1939 play *Johnson over Jordan*. 'Everyman' Robert Johnson has died suddenly in his 50s and has had to re-live his remembered life at a way-station that is called the Inn at the End of the World. It has come time now for him to leave everything, including his most precious memories, and move on to ... whatever is next.

Imagine an unwritten scene at the end of Thornton Wilder's play *Our Town*, in which the sitting dead, unsure of their future and constantly musing, with increasing detachment, over the thwarted lives they left behind, are finally summoned to move onwards. That is what is happening now at the conclusion of *Johnson over Jordan*. Priestley took the bold step of actually writing the scene, or at least a part of it, that Wilder left to our imagination.

> JOHNSON *(With deep emotion.)*
> I have been a foolish, greedy, and ignorant man;
> Yet I have had my time beneath the sun and stars;
> I have known the returning strength and sweetness of the seasons,

Blossom on the branch and the ripening of fruit,

...

The earth is nobler than the world we have built upon it;

...

The world still shifting, dark, half-evil.
But what have I done that I should have a better world,
Even though there is in me something that will not rest
Until it sees Paradise...?

...

THE FIGURE *(Gravely.)*
Robert Johnson, it is time now.

...

JOHNSON *(Now with his overcoat on, holding his hat and bag...)*
For Thine is the kingdom, the power, and the glory ... and
God bless Jill and Freda and Richard ... and all my friends—
and—and—everybody ... for ever and ever ... Amen.
... *As JOHNSON still stands there, hesitating, the light on
the FIGURE fades, and then the whole staircase disappears,
leaving JOHNSON alone. He looks very small, forlorn, for
now the whole stage has been opened up to its maximum size,
and there is nothing there but JOHNSON. ... JOHNSON looks
about him, shivering a little, and turning up the collar of his
coat. And now there is a rapidly growing intense blue light; the
high curtains have gone at the back, where it is bluer and bluer;
until at last we see the glitter of stars in space, and against them
the curve of the world's rim. As the brass blares out triumphantly
and the drums roll and the cymbals clash, JOHNSON, wearing
his bowler hat and carrying his bag, slowly turns and walks
towards that blue space and the shining constellations, and the
curtain comes down and the play is done.*

If J. B. Priestley is right, and I think we can confirm what he says just
by gazing at the stars over a quiet beach at night, we are swallowed
after death by the whole of Eternity and enter into a feeling of
oneness with it. The oneness we sought, usually in another person, is
provided now in full. It becomes organic to our souls. It is no longer

conditional nor contingent. It is the Fourth Dimension of the world.

The love we tried to find in life, and sometimes did, hopefully in one abiding human being who loved us back, is the same in quality as, just deeper and less distracted than, the Love behind the universe. We go to that Love entirely reconciled to our chronic mistakes, on innumerable fronts and with uncountable people, by the forgiveness of God accomplished by the death of Jesus on the Cross. Like the character Johnson, who said goodbye in the play to his thoughtless selfishness, his petty temptations, and his much regretted failures to love in fact, we travel light. We are not, like the ghosts of the skittering souls outside Scrooge's window, bound to "the chains they wrought in life." That part has been taken care of. Johnson reconciled to himself, Johnson at peace with his past, Johnson now enabled to face the One who is "of purer eyes than to behold evil, and canst not look on iniquity" (Habakkuk 1:13), Johnson absolved—that man is ready to move forward, as are we.

But there is even more. We can, in fact, from ancient inspiration, say more.

"Tattoo You" (Rolling Stones, 1981)

Beloved, we are God's children now; it does not yet appear what we shall be, but we know that when he appears, we shall be like him, for we shall see him as he is.

(I John 3:2)

And I saw no temple therein: for the Lord God Almighty and the Lamb are the temple of it. ... And he shewed me a pure river of water of life, clear as crystal ... And they shall see his face; and his name shall be in their foreheads.

(Revelation 21:22; 22:1, 4)

Traditional Christians—I am one—usually wince a little when people talk about "the God within," or "the God part of you." We want to keep the distinction between the creature—me—and the Creator—Him. The reason for this is our own experience, for we *tried* to save ourselves apart from God but we failed. Our world came crashing down despite continual 'small-time' efforts to prop it up. It was *God* who saved us when we crashed and burned, not we ourselves. It was *God's* agency, not our own, that came to our aid. We can swear to that.

But we also found out that the love we craved, by way of a unitive connection, involved a recognition, unconscious at first but almost all-engrossing in the long run, of the One in the other person whom we loved or desired to love. We identified with the character Jean Valjean in *Les Mis*, who sang "To love another person is to see the face of God."

Then soul music and rock 'n' roll came along to enforce the fact, as in the Temptations chorus from 1967, "You're my everything, you're my everything, you're my everything, you're my everything." The songs—as opposed to this rational, deflating world—told us a truth about ourselves. We were looking for Somebody, but that Somebody came in the form of somebody.

On the one hand, we were saved by Grace, "not of our own doing, it is the gift of God" (Ephesians 2:8). On the other hand, the *actual* saving was a little hard to distinguish from the well-like eyes, the shining face, and the simple reaching out of a single other human being.

This "slight momentary" (II Corinthians 4:17) disconnect will be resolved at death. On the one hand, you have been blessedly separated, by the completely unearned, counterintuitive Mercy of God, from your false self. That 'critter' has been left prowling on the earth; or better, "in pieces on the ground" (James Taylor, 1970), somewhat like a balloon that has been popped and is now the size of a small child's finger. You, on the other hand, the true you, got off just in time. The whirly bird lifted off, and you were taken up, like a U.S. Army Medivac helicopter on the Mekong Delta in the summer of '69. You don't have to go back there, and you will never see 'old sourpuss' again!

Now you are "Reunited" (Peaches and Herb, 1978) with the One. And you shall be like Him, for you shall see Him as He is (I John 3:2). And that odd feeling you have now of profoundest solidarity—

entirely unfamiliar to the false self—will have been caused by the oneness with God that you have 100% in common with all the other still 'shadowy' true selves all around you. "And they shall see his face; and his name shall be in their foreheads" (Revelation 22:4). You will get used to it, quickly; but it will be a "New Feeling" (Talking Heads, 1977) if ever there was one. It will also be permanent.

When you 'pass on'—a verb that's recently been euphemistically shortened, almost overnight, to 'pass'—you *break up* with your old, grabby, crabby, id-ego-super-ego self by means of the forgiveness of God in the face of your pride-less repentance. You will never see that self again. You are now "different," as Jimmy Webb wrote in "Where I Am Going"—"you're just like me." Your divorce from the tie that bound—the continuing love affair you had with 'yourself,' the least frangible of all "soul-ties"—is final. Now you are standing within an infinite crowd of true selves, all of whom look the same, not from an intrinsic uniformity, but from the one divine imprint of the Love-attribute that is the true soul-tie. "Faith, hope, and love abide, these three; and the greatest of these is love" (I Cor. 13:13).

Here we are at the limits of what words can describe. Here, we see "through a glass darkly" (I Cor. 13:12). But you can be sure that in the "Sea of Love" (Joe Simon, 1972), when we see God "face to face" (I Cor. 13:12), it's going to be "a whole new world" (*Aladdin*, 1992)!

"Plasticine Porters with Looking Glass Ties" (The Beatles, 1967)

On a clear but cold afternoon in January 2015, I was sitting watching some ducks on a pond in Washington Park in Denver. Then came one of those waking visions that you have and you never forget. You know the kind.

In my mind's eye I saw my Mary 'checking into' Heaven. She saw me, too, although I was separated from her by a thick yellow plasticine curtain. She was standing and being efficiently processed as if she were checking into a well run hotel. I, on the other hand, on 'my' side of the plasticine curtain, was seated with my head in my hands.

In the scene I saw, Mary was worried that I wasn't with her. I could see her arguing with the receptionist, as if to say, "What about Paul? I can't go in without Paul." It was apparent that I was in a different situation than she, and that she was qualified to go in but I would have to stay. She looked with such love and deeply felt concern on her face. But there was nothing she could do. I was 'on my own.'

Then, while she was looking at me with unforgettable sorrow—for she could do nothing to help me—she began to 'break up.' What I mean is, she began to dissolve into particles of light. Even within the vision I remembered a 1980 *Hammer House of Horror* television episode from England entitled "Visitor from the Grave." At the end of that episode, a dead woman reappears, in this case, to haunt her persecutors in life, and after she gets her justice, she 'breaks up,' like Mary in my waking dream, into a thousand shimmering pieces of light.

In my case, my ever-loving Mary, who could do nothing more for me but was herself ready and qualified to take up residence in *The White Hotel* (D. M. Thomas, 1981), also began to break up into shimmering light. I, comfortless and completely alone, was held back, seated with head in hands, behind a thick, worn, yellow plasticine sheet.

"Yes, I'm Ready"
(Barbara Mason, 1965)

Boomer! I say, Boomer!! JOHNSON! Deceased Citizens of *Our Town*! Don't end up like me in that waking dream.

Fortunately, I no longer identify with the 'me' within the January 2015 dream. For reasons I trust, I no longer see myself as that forlorn character behind a plasticine curtain within a "Tangerine Dream." But I did then. And it is the close definition of hell, what we used to call "separation from God."

O Boomer, this is your wakeup call.

A wonderful man, just turned 81, said to me, "When you cross over into your 80s, it's a pretty terrible thing. You simply *have* to start thinking about 'Where I Am Going.'"

I am trying, through this book, to get you to start a little earlier than that.

After age 60—and with some people you know it happened before their 60s—your body is a lot more vulnerable to "sudden floods and fall of waters" (*Richard III*, Act IV, Scene IV). The coronavirus has taught us that—again.

Plus, if you get really sick, they'll 'put you under' in no time flat, depriving you of the necessary conscious reflection, like my Ossining priest friend was mercifully given at the end, to cut the knot of the false self. Do you really want to 'pass' in a mental state so drugged and soporific that you can't even attempt the work of final resolution?

START EARLY. GET A HOLD OF YOURSELF. REPENT AND PRAY.

Or, in oldest, newest words,

"Look up, and lift up your heads; for your redemption draweth nigh" (Luke 21:28). ✛✛✛

"Making Plans for Nigel"— Envisioning the Terms of a Boomer's Life of Peace and Hope

B oomers spend a lot of time with widows and widowers. Many of us *are* widows and widowers. And most of the rest of us will be one or the other pretty soon.

"I'm so Tired of Being Alone, I'm so Tired of Being Alone" (Al Green, 1971)

What I hear from my fellow Boomers and used to hear often during decades of prior parish ministry, is something like this: "It's the lone-liness I hate. Sure, I have gotten used to it a little. But everything feels pretty gray right now; and to tell you the truth, I'm ready to go."

Each of the sexes seems to add a little something extra to the lament.

Some of the women add, "After [Bill] died, I didn't feel like I had much to live for anymore. Guess taking care of him gave me a kind of reason for living. It's not that I long for death, no. It's just that I don't feel like I have much to live for. The grandchildren, yes, of course; but most of them are far away—and my son's a little touchy."

Some of the men add—actually, they rarely say it in words, but they say it in (non-)action: "I read a lot now and watch the news. Probably drink too much, too. I do try to make the early service most Sundays. Oh, and there's also Lloyd, my old friend from school. Lloyd's not very well, but we try to talk once a week if we can. My brother I don't talk to. Wish I did. And this old house is getting pretty messy, I'll admit. I sure don't want to go anywhere else, though." Again, the latter confession is seldom in words, but I observe it.

Jerome K. Jerome

This Englishman with the funny name wrote a famous short novel entitled *Two Men in a Boat* (1889). I want to retitle it, the reader will know, *We Are All in the Same Boat*. Everyone, and now especially Boomers because we have reached that age, is in the same boat. Our bodies are losing ground, our minds are not what they were, our contemporaries have begun to leave the building—"(Don't Fear) The Reaper" (Blue Oyster Cult, 1976)—and many of our conceptions of what is good and valuable seem no longer to apply, or even interest us very much. We are, as it were, *outliving* the problems of our prior values. Everything is either all starting to look the same, or it's all looking pretty stark, and awful.

Where is the hope for our future? Can we reach the end of the last third of our lives with something to live for, something to go on? Say it again, PZ. Or at least sum it up in brief: What does Mockingbird faith mean for Boomers?

Abreactive Listening

This conclusion to *A Handbook of Hope for Boomers* envisions the terms of a Boomer life that is characterized by peace and hope. It envisions what a Boomer's peaceful and hopeful life can consist of—especially in terms of outward-reaching, future-oriented engagement.

For years I visited dozens of nursing homes and retirement communities. During those visits I would see small armies of aging people watching episodes of *Jeopardy* in 'serried ranks' of wheelchairs, their heads mostly nodding in half sleep. That is not a caricature, and it is not an overstatement. I used to wish that those sorry residents' adult children could see their parents now. I also wished the grown children could see *themselves* as they would probably look in 25 or 30 years.

You can walk up and down the corridors of an everyday nursing home and be literally almost pulled down by people wanting to talk to you. And it's not just senile dementia and mental illness. The people you see—like you and me probably, in a decade or two—have *no one to talk to*.

Read Stephen King's *The Green Mile* (1999) for an empathic and accurate description of your future 'fate' in a 'retirement community.' The fine and even noble protagonist, a prison guard who once encountered a literal Christ-figure in the person of a prisoner on death row, subsists now in a nursing home. He is a man of acute perception and massive experience, but who is now consigned to dodging from and also bartering with mean, petty, and unfeeling attendant staff. This good man, who is as altruistic and loyal as a person could possibly be, ends up having to stash little desserts from the cafeteria under his shirt, and using every trick in the trade he once knew as a prison guard, to fool the LPNs for the sake of a little walk outside.

Now just imagine that the poor soul who is gesturing at you with both arms extended as you walk past her tiny shared bedroom on the way-too-brightly-lit corridor of her nursing home is that good man, or your mother and father. Or you!

As a Boomer, "get thee to a nunnery" (*Hamlet*, Act III, Scene I). Which is another way of saying, find someone who will listen to you. Don't put it off any longer. You have a lot to say. You have a whole lifetime to abreact. Like the quiet sufferers in Taylor Caldwell's novel, find someone to listen to you. It is not easy to find such a willing person, but it is not impossible. There are things you need to get off your chest. This is not an 'optional extra.' If you do not find someone to listen to you soon, you will "not go gentle into that good night" (Dylan Thomas). Rather, you will go kicking and screaming—and not just from massive untrammeled resistance, but simply because you are not ready to go. This mustn't happen.

To be quite concrete, pray for a listener to come alongside. They probably never will "in the natural". But God can send someone—in the supernatural! Pray for a listener to find you. Mary's and my faith tells us that your listener is "Round Every Corner" (Petula Clark, 1965). I am praying for your listener to come!

The 'Listenee' Becomes the Listener

Something you notice in life—and it doesn't have to take Martin Luther to teach you—is that a truly generous action, an action undertaken for someone else's benefit without your factoring in what it can *do* for you, is usually spontaneous, unplanned, and, in some inward way, a response to something generous that someone else has done for your benefit. In other words, heartfelt and unconstrained love is usually a *response* to someone else's loving you.

You don't really *decide,* through some long dialogue with the will, to do something altruistic. The thought just comes to you. The 'backstory' to your thought typically hinges on a prior gesture in your direction from somebody else. This is why we never tire of quoting I John 4:19: "We love, because God first loved us."

Bob Dylan said something like this in his song "Saving Grace" (1980): "Wherever I am welcome is where I'll be." My security of belovedness is preface, in almost every case, to my loving —and welcoming—another.

Here is how the Lutheran theologian Karl Holl put it in his book *The Reconstruction of Morality* (1921):

> Luther laid the greatest emphasis of all on the fact that everything must be done freely and joyfully. ... Whatever action does not arise spontaneously from within, but is forced

for a specific purpose at a particular moment, will not last.

...

The Spirit propels people so that they cannot do otherwise; and yet there is not even the slightest sense of compulsion. Luther declares that it is nonsense to say that the justified ought to do good; they do good as naturally as a tree bears its fruit.

Here we come to the first of the new 'terms' of a Boomer's life of peace and hope.

If you are a Boomer who has been listened to and your preoccupying memories have been abreacted, you are now fit to become a listener to your countless fellow Boomers who are living under the pressure of mental preoccupations that are so stultifying that it is as if the key to their 'safe room' was thrown away and is now irrecoverable.

Did you ever see the episode of the revived *Twilight Zone* in which a paranoid man hears that a nuclear attack is coming—in about 20 minutes—so he descends to his 'safe room,' a high-tech bomb shelter he constructed in the basement without telling anyone, including his wife, and locked himself in? The episode was called "Shelter Skelter" and was televised in 1987. His wife, however, and their small children are visiting her sister in another town, and he is upset to the highest pitch that they will die, up on the surface, and he will live. He is not a bad man.

But then it turns out the nuclear attack is more or less a false alarm. When the man's family returns, relieved beyond words, there is no sign of their husband and father. Because he buried the entrance to the safe room so carefully and anonymously, no one knew it was there. The bereaved, mystified wife and her children move away. Later, the house is bulldozed to make way for a peace memorial(!). At the end of the episode, the poor man sits alone in his underground chamber, with supplies enough for a lifetime, having no idea that his wife and children, who think him mysteriously dead or disappeared, are up on the surface world, which ... goes about its business again.

I believe that many Boomers are buried alive like the man in

"Shelter Skelter." They are buried within frozen pasts and memories, and solidified habits of coping. Like the 'hero' of "Shelter Skelter," they need to get out! Their buried selves, which are doing neither themselves nor anyone else any good, need to be exhumed, released, *lit* again by the sun. And you, dear abreacted Boomer, are the only sun that many of your fellow Boomers are ever going to get.

Become a listener.

Stop Being a 'Moderate' in Religion

Remember that article from the *Wall Street Journal*, which said that the 'moderately' religious are in decline in the U.S.A., but the 'intensely' religious are on the upswing?

Reports of the slow death of Christianity in this country are exaggerated. Or rather, the rapid increase of non-denominational evangelical and Pentecostal churches, especially among young people, is underreported. Take a road trip from Maine to San Diego! You will see almost as many billboards advertising evangelical/Spirit-filled church plants as you will for trial lawyers. (Though maybe not quite as many.) Try it. Even in the Bay Area, even in suburban Baltimore, even in Amesbury, Massachusetts—they're everywhere. The Spring crocuses of serious Christianity are blooming all around us.

Another way of putting this is to underline for Boomers: *Open yourself up to the Supernatural Power of God.*

I got a sincere but somewhat pathetic prayer request from an old friend last year, asking me to pray for her friend's stage-four breast cancer. My friend asked me to pray for good medical care for the person, for patience and endurance for the person's husband, for a sound mind among her family that would know when it was time to "pull the plug," and for a loving exchange of ideas concerning the inevitable funeral. I wrote back, asking if the possibility of praying for remission in this case were on the table. She wrote back saying that it had not come up. There you have it. I only asked.

Then later, during the coronavirus pandemic, I received a series of prayers from the chaplains of the Episcopal prep school I attended. Not one of the prayers included a single note of supplication for the virus itself to be restrained or for healing to be given to any who had contracted it.

If you have been touched by the Supernatural Power of God, O freshly empowered Boomer, then you can become a charming channel, a flowing sluice, for witness. If something happened to you, in other words, then it could happen to somebody else.

I used to be diffident about praying for the remission or healing of a physical illness, let alone of a mental incapacity or disturbance. I would 'cover myself'—and the God who had ordained me in 1975—by praying for the sufferer's acceptance and serenity much more often than for God's intervention and victory.

I was wrong.

Now I wish I could follow Pastor Paula around during her once-a-month Power Nights in Apopka, Florida, carrying one of those little shawls or blankets—I still haven't figured out what they are—that her assistants put on the people for whom Pastor prays and they fall back on the ground. Or perhaps I could hold her jar of anointing oil, with which she has been extremely liberal when it came to praying for me! Greasy hands, fingers, and face; and I love it.

The point is, you want to give out and give back what you have been given. As Karl Holl would say, the natural response to God's Grace in your life, which is to give it to others, is uncompelled, completely free, and blissfully extemporary.

End Zone

We are edging up to the zone of the last and most important point in this handbook for Boomers, this pharmacy of peace and hope for people over 60. The ending phase of life reveals more and more the magnetic attraction of archaeological memories of connection. God bless you if you are still able to be with "the wife of your youth" (Proverbs 5:18). That is about the greatest gift a person can ever have.

It is also rare. You and she/he have shared so much together—everything, really. Our life together, it's been "Our Movie" (Glen Campbell, 1988), "Directed by two, / Produced for free / ... You see, it's written in our hearts." Yet all of us will eventually lose even that. "Our Movie," if she predeceases me, will become, at least in the coda of it, "My Movie." One way or another, one of us will probably die alone. Alone, that is, but for God.

What this book has tried to bring out is the zeal for connection with which we are born and with which we live out our entire planetary course. That fusion-hope, to put it in strongest terms, is our "Stairway to Heaven," as in the O'Jays' song. But it is preliminary. It is partial and incomplete. And it is passing away.

It is actually "The Shape of Things (to Come)" (Yardbirds, 1966). Guess we could call it a pledge to be redeemed later, in full. Through these "soul-ties" of life, God "Dedicates My Life to You" (The Dramatics, 1973). The wedding ring that was placed on the fourth finger of my left hand over 46 years ago by Mary Cappleman in the First United Methodist Church of Winter Garden, Florida, is a pledge. But the object of that pledge is the never-ending love of God. And "When I Die" (Motherlode, 1970), "though this body be destroyed, yet shall I see God: whom I shall see for myself, and mine eyes shall behold, and not as a stranger" (Job 19:26-27).

What I have meant to do by emphasizing the romantic connection, which the Top-40 songs overwhelmingly affirm, is that we are able to see here and now a qualitative 'first fruits' of the "Love that wilt not let me go" (George Matheson, 1882).

The night so long ago when I first heard Mary out! The night I knew she heard *me* out. God was there, subsisting between us. We needed to look no further. And what we shall, each and both, gain when we die, is the ultimate unbreakable unity, both between ourselves and with God, which is the heartbeat of life. Our ultimate unbreakable unity is with God and derives from God.

Sometimes people say that life is an end in itself. What they mean is that the sheer act of breathing and 'being here' is a wonder, and is splendid on its own terms. I disagree. I know what they mean, and certainly a pure clean breath on a "Rocky Mountain High"

(John Denver, 1972) is revivifying and superb. But I would also say that only the life that is a connected soul-tie with God, and the unsurpassed heart for unity with God that lies beneath and behind all human aspirations for relationship, is really life.

Peace at the Last

J. M. Barrie wrote *Peter Pan* (1904). Few writers have understood better than Barrie the enduring 'spell' of our childhood over us as we grow into adults.

J.M. Barrie also understood death. He grasped especially the possibility of a dying person's real peace at the end of their life. His grasp of it came about because he had witnessed the death of his mother, who died within a most serene and peaceful state of mind.

Here is J. M. Barrie's description of the death of his mother:

> They knew now that she was dying... then for some time she talked of the long lovely life that had been hers, and of Him to whom she owed it. She said good-bye to them all, and at last turned her face to the side of the bed where her best-beloved had lain, and for over an hour she prayed. They only caught the words now and again, and the last they heard were "God" and "love". I think God was smiling when He took her to Him, as He had so often smiled at her during those seventy-six years.

Such is my hope for the last third of your life, O dearly beloved Boomer. Let alone my own. ✢✢✢

A Boomer's Confession and Credo

"Say It Isn't So"
I'm sorry I got caught up in pursuits, from my 20s through my 60s, that didn't give me what I was looking for.

"Where's the Playground, Suzie"
I'm sorry I didn't realize I was shadow-boxing nine-tenths of the time.

"Looking for Love in All the Wrong Places"
I'm sorry I looked for secondary love when what I needed was primary love. I didn't know. When it came to love, I was a "Silly, Silly Fool" (Dusty Springfield, 1970).

"Will It Go Round in Circles?"
This merry-go-round has stopped! My body's failing, my mind's not what it was, and my whole world feels like it's quietly slipping off its main frame. (It is!)

"Corona, Corona"
The entire structure of my fretful, disappointed life is starting to feel like the onset of a personal apocalypse.

"Are You Ready?"

Listen, please: I am *so sorry* that this last third of my life is taking me by surprise. I am NOT ready for death. *Je répète*, NOT.

"Tell Me"

I understand I need someone to talk to. Soon and at length. I have kept so much down. Now I think I'm ready to blow "Sky High" (Jigsaw, 1975). This is urgent.

"The Power of Love"

I want to believe in the Supernatural Power of God. And I don't care if people think I've gone off the rails. "I'm Coming Out" (Diana Ross, 1980) and am believing for my miracle!

"Where Love Has Gone"

I believe that God's Love, in Jesus Christ our Lord, is final, lasting, one-way, absolving, perfect, and perfectly satisfying. Other than that, most of what has passed for love in my life was "Just a Mirage" (Smokey Robinson and the Miracles, 1967). I want the Real Thing and I want it bad.

"Drowning in a Sea of Love"

I believe that's OK. It's OK to drown in the Sea of Love. That's a 'death' I can handle. "Give It To Me" (J. Geils Band, 1973), and I'll be fine forever.

And in the life everlasting. Amen.

APPENDIX ONE

Dedicated Listening from Mary Zahl

AS I READ the proofs for Paul's book, my main question was, "Where are these readers going to find someone to listen to them?"

On reflection, it might be easier than you think to find someone to listen to you. As someone who has been leading workshops for the last twenty-five years on Christian Listening, as taught by Canon Anne Long of the Acorn Christian Healing Trust in England, I have witnessed countless people experience the power of listening and being listened to. Sadly, I see very few good listeners in daily interactions; most conversations are simply people taking turns talking. However, when given five or ten or fifteen minutes of dedicated time and a partner who is willing to participate, almost anyone can follow a few simple guidelines for good listening that is far more effective for healing than most would suspect.

What am I suggesting, based on my experience, is this:

1. Find someone you trust to keep your confidence. This can be a spouse, if you have one, or a close friend. It can be someone you know at church. The person does not need to be a trained counselor or an ordained person. *Simply someone who is willing to dedicate 30 minutes of time to listening and being listened to without*

comment or questions. Note: this is not the same as a conversation. It may feel 'formal' or awkward; that is normal. Nevertheless, my experience is that this Dedicated Listening experience is far more effective in healing than hours of informal conversation.

2. Find a time and place where neither of you will be distracted. Set your phone on airplane mode. The Listener will need a timer, however. Decide how long your listening time will be, with a minimum of five minutes, but no more than fifteen at the outset, and set a timer. You can adjust for subsequent sessions, once you have mastered the exercise.

3. Decide who will be the first Speaker. Choose a topic to discuss that touches on something that has disturbed you recently, or something about which you need to sort through your feelings. As the Speaker you can say as much or as little as you choose in the time allotted.

4. The Listener will give full attention to the Speaker, but *not say anything.* You can nod, say 'mmm', or if necessary, 'would you like to say more?'

5. When the Speaker has finished, ask the following questions in turn. After each reply, the Listener repeats back what the Speaker has said, using the Speaker's words, but *without interpretation.*

   • *Of all that you have been saying, what do you think is most important?*
   • *Is there anything you would like to do about what you have said?*

6. After the first Speaker has used her allotted time and answered the questions, the roles are reversed.

From my experience with this exercise, the comments after both participants have had the chance to listen and be listened to, are invariably, "I can't remember the last time anyone listened to me that well." Or, " I was amazed how much I was able to say and how deep I was able to go in that short amount of time." For the listeners, it is almost always, "I had no idea what a poor listener I am. I wanted to jump in so often, that I realize I seldom really listen to anyone."

There are a few principles in good listening, which, when followed, almost always enable graceful healing to take place—the kind of healing Paul has talked about in this book.

These include:

1. Look the Speaker in the eye, and give him your full attention.

2. No interrupting, ever. Most people listen with the intent to reply, which is not really listening at all.

3. No advice giving, in spite of how much insight you think you have. In response to the second question (above), you show that you trust the person *to give herself advice* which she is infinitely more likely to follow than your wisest, most loving intention. Your advice will almost always set up a rebellious reaction, and it often falls into the category of your 'needing to help', when that is not being solicited.

4. Do not tell your own story in response to theirs. You may think you are expressing empathy, but you are simply redirecting the conversation back to yourself and, in effect, silencing the Speaker.

5. No asking of informational questions. They have nothing to do with what the Speaker is trying to say and will cause the conversation to stay at the surface when your goal is to enable emotional depth so that healing can take place.

6. Do not minimize or spiritualize. This communicates, "I do not take your pain seriously." Or, more likely, the Speaker's pain is making you (the Listener) anxious. Or, perhaps you hear an inner voice about 'witnessing,' telling you to quote scripture. These responses are about the Listener, not the Speaker.

7. Develop a comfort level with silence. Only if it becomes awkward for the Speaker, you might say, "Would you like to say more about that?"

8. What the Speaker says is confidential, always.

I hope you will try this. To quote the letter from James, *'be quick to listen, slow to speak, slow to anger'* (James 1:19). So much wisdom in those words! And, so much potential for healing and peace.

Books and Media to Help Boomers Find Peace and Hope

This is a list of books and media to which I have referred in the text. It is alphabetized by title.

Adam Bede (1859) by George Eliot
Eliot's story of thwarted, wayward love and also married, Christian love is as touching an expression of what brings men and women together for life, as well as what separates them, as any novel in the world. Moreover, its description of a young female evangelist is pitch perfect and simply lovely. Dinah Morris is one of the most appealing Christian characters in all of literature.

The Black Fox (1950) by Gerald Heard
An astonishing supernatural novel about demon-possession taking over an ambitious Church of England cathedral canon. The resolution is hopeful and deep. There are also delightful references to liturgical churchmanship that will make you smile, especially if you are, like me, a Protestant churchman.

Bright Flows the River (1978) by Taylor Caldwell
This novel concerns a mid-career businessman with a long-standing marriage and adult children, who has suffered a complete nervous breakdown with no apparent cause. It narrates his past, his present, and his (finally) hopeful future.

The Christians (2015) by Lucas Hnath
This play presents a successful evangelical pastor who morphs into a theological liberal, causing consternation in his wife and disillusionment in his associate minister. Yet they have the last word. There is a shattering deathbed scene towards the end of the play that confirms the afterlife.

Citizen Kane (1941)
Orson Welles's famous movie concerns the death and rise of Charles Foster Kane, a character based on the real-life William Randolph Hearst. *Citizen Kane* illustrates poignantly but also grimly what it is to die a bad death.

Divine Madness: Archetypes of Romantic Love (1990) by John R. Haule
This is the best book I have read concerning the "soul-tie," even though it never uses the term.

The Genius and the Goddess (1955) by Aldous Huxley
This story of an outlandishly unhappy marriage and family, with its speculative, metaphysical conclusion, is total food for thought concerning the secret inward causations behind outward struggles. With a dash of English understatement, Huxley delineates the difference in practice between his characters' true selves and their false selves.

Grandmother and the Priests (1963) by Taylor Caldwell
A collection of imaginative, moving short stories concerning the pastoral lives of Roman Catholic parish priests in England, Scotland, and Wales. Good deaths abound, as do bad; and the author's Christian insight concerning the hiddenness of people's true feelings is memorable and illuminating.

The Green Mile (1999) by Stephen King
The admirable hero of this novel, a death row prison guard, meets an authentic Christ-figure. Much later, the hero has become an acquiescent yet wily resident in a fairly low-end nursing home. His life has a good outcome, though, "Against All Odds" (Phil Collins, 1981).

Johnson Over Jordan (1939) by J. B. Priestley
In this play concerning the afterlife of everyman Robert Johnson, the hero must confront his entire false self, as well as the elements of his true self which carried the love and the loves of his life. The dramatist, J. B. Priestley, asked Benjamin Britten to write the incidental music for his play. The result was a dazzling work of religious introspection in both words and music.

The Last Adam (1933) by James Gould Cozzens
This entire book, which was also made into a Hollywood movie directed by John Ford and starring Will Rogers, i.e., *Doctor Bull* (1933), boils down to a two-page section at the end which diagnoses the birth, gestation, apparent triumph, and ultimate failure of 'moderate religion' within mainline Protestantism. Its author grew up in the bosom of Northeastern cultural Episcopalianism, and no one has ever said it better than he, in this odd, penetrating novel.

The Listener (1960) by Taylor Caldwell
It's not that I worship Taylor Caldwell! It is just that her religious and pastoral interests, hung upon the clothes of an acute imagination, make great ideas accessible to the everyday reader, let alone to yours truly. This book sums up the transformational power that is carried by good listening.

Listening (1990) by Anne Long
This is the Godfather of contemporary books on listening. It is so good, and so fine. It is also crying out, while the author yet liveth, for a new and revised second edition.

Little Boy (2015)
If there is a single movie that I would recommend more than all others to the readers of this book, in light of the hope embodied within Christian faith, it would be *Little Boy*. The *Village Voice* devoted almost an entire page to attacking the film, but that is probably to the film's credit. If you are discouraged in literally any area of your life, see *Little Boy*. (Oh, and please don't be discouraged by the 'Hallmark Card'-ish narration at the start. It is almost enough to make you want to turn the movie off. But it gets over soon.)

Madea's Family Reunion (2006)
Tyler Perry has made several movies out of his Gospel plays that feature the outrageous and hilarious character whom he himself plays, Madea. This one features Cicely Tyson as "Aunt Myrtle," whose Christian faith is the key to the film.

Manhunter (1986)
This hip psychological thriller from the 1980s was directed by Michael Mann, the creator of *Miami Vice*. It is a tale of dark empathy, by which the detective gets his man. This is human nature up close. "In-A-Gadda-Da-Vida," too!

"Nervous Man in a Four Dollar Room" (1960)
Rod Serling wrote this teleplay for the second season of *The Twilight Zone*. It posits two persons within one 'hero,' and carries it off perfectly. I like to show "Nervous Man in a Four Dollar Room" to church groups and others in order to illustrate the transition from "false self" to "true self."

"Nightmare" (1963)
This episode of *The Outer Limits* depicts the captivity of a squad of "Earthmen" captured by the alien Ebonites in an interplanetary war. "Nightmare" is 'monist' because it parabolizes a benign intention behind an unspeakable present.

Number Seven, Queer Street (1966) by Margery Lawrence
The English author of this collection of supernatural ghost stories
had a lot to say about life after death, guilt and loss retained with
great cost from this present life, and the deliverance embodied in
Christian symbols and insights. Highly recommended.

Outward Bound (1923) by Sutton Vane
Sutton Vane's unforgettable play presents a group of people who
have just died and find themselves on an ocean liner conveying
them to Final Judgment. *Outward Bound* also presents a couple in
romantic love who are both mistaken *and* correct. The first movie
version (1930), starring Leslie Howard, is technically a little creaky,
but absolutely true to its inspired source.

The Philly Sound 1966-1976: Kenny Gamble and Leon Huff (1997)
The universal longing for romantic love, the all-consuming search
to find the binding "soul-tie," exists within almost every track of
this outstanding collection of Philadelphia Soul hits. From the Soul
Survivors to the O'Jays to Teddy Pendergrass, it is all here: the hunger for the one that functions like the One.

What is Protestantism? (1965)
This anthology of short essays, letters, and stories was put together
by the Evangelical Episcopalian Walter Russell Bowie. It contains
Sir J.M. Barrie's reminiscence of his mother's death.

The Reconstruction of Morality (English edition, 1979) by Karl Holl
This is the masterpiece of Protestant ethical reflection. It is an
anatomy of what Martin Luther called "free and spontaneous
action": works of un-self-conscious love that are rooted in the prior
love of God—or, as is often experienced on this planet, the prior
love of another person.

Sacred Rhythms: Arranging our Lives for Spiritual Transformation
(2006) by Ruth Haley Barton
This short book seeks to focus the reader on one thing: answering the

core but often unconscious question you have inside you that actually motivates most of what you do and most of how you live. There is
also a series of video talks by the author, which can accompany it.

She and Allan (1921) by H. Rider Haggard
Allan Quatermain, Haggard's mourning hero, sets off on a quest
to find the answer to his urgent question concerning the afterlife.
After some to-ing and fro-ing, and after a decisive encounter with
Ayesha, "She-Who-Must-Be-Obeyed," Allan finds what he is look-
ing for—in part.

"Static" (1961)
Charles Beaumont scripted this episode of *The Twilight Zone*,
which presents a lonely, regretful man who is given the gift of rec-
reating his emotional past, which in turn creates a new and hopeful
future. Dean Jagger is wonderful as the hero; and Carmen Mathews
is, too, as his lost-and-found other.

Tight Corners in Pastoral Counselling (1981) by Frank Lake
This next-to-last book by the genius himself is full of insights for
pastoral care.
      But the crown jewel of the book is Dr. Lake's chapter entitled
"Infatuation and the Divine." It is almost as good as the Haule
above, but is committedly, inspiringly Christian.

The Tommyknockers (1987) by Stephen King
This is one of his best, because it presents a perfect metaphor for
the power of the past to determine *everything*, while at the same
time offering one man, a not-so-recovering alcoholic, the incred-
ible chance to save the world. King's novel was also made into an
excellent made-for-television miniseries in 1993.

The War of the Worlds (1953)
This hopeful and pervasively religious 'take' on H. G. Wells's novel
is one of the wonders of Hollywood's sci-fi Golden Age. The three
churches to which the hero flees at the climax are regarded by the

filmmakers as the most positive, comforting, and hopeful sanctuaries possible; and when the evangelical pastor of the third and final church prays for a miracle, it happens!

You're Not Listening (2019) by Kate Murphy
A passionate, secular call to better listening. Highly recommended. Read, if you don't read anything else in her book, Kate Murphy's account, at the end, of the Basilica of Our Lady of San Juan del Valle in San Juan, Texas. There, the office of listening inspires lines almost as long as those for ... a Trump rally.

Note that all of these television episodes, movies, novels, and CDs are easy to find and are available through the Internet.

APPENDIX THREE

A Boomer Playlist

These are almost all Top 40 songs, featured in *A Handbook of Hope for Boomers*. They are popular evidence for the thesis of the book. They are also all great songs! Each of them is easily available.

"Beginnings" (Chicago, 1969)

"Betcha By Golly, Wow" (The Stylistics, 1971)

"Brandy (You're a Fine Girl)" (Looking Glass, 1972)

"Drowning in the Sea of Love" (Joe Simon, 1972)

"God Only Knows" (The Beach Boys, 1966)

"In-A-Gadda-Da-Vida" (Iron Butterfly, 1968)

"Kind of a Drag" (The Buckinghams, 1967)

"Love Epidemic" (The Trammps, 1975)

"The Love I Lost" (Harold Melvin & the Blue Notes, 1973)

"Love is Blue" (Paul Mauriat, 1968)

"Never Can Say Goodbye" (The Jackson 5, 1971)

"Only the Strong Survive" (Jerry Butler, 1969)

"The Power of Love" (Frankie Goes to Hollywood, 1984)

"The Power of Love" (Huey Lewis and the News, 1985)

"Reelin' in the Years" (Steely Dan, 1972)

"Reflections of My Life" (Marmalade, 1970)

"Rice Is Nice" (The Lemon Pipers, 1968)

"Sideshow" (Blue Magic, 1974)

"Somebody to Love" (Jefferson Airplane, 1967)

"Stairway to Heaven" (The O'Jays, 1975)

"Tighter, Tighter" (Alive N Kickin, 1970)

"Too Busy Thinking About My Baby" (Marvin Gaye, 1969)

"When I Die" (Motherlode, 1970)

"Where I Am Going" (Glen Campbell, 1991)

"Without the One You Love (Life Is Not Worthwhile)"
    (The Four Tops, 1964)

"You Saved My Soul" (Burton Cummings, 1997)

✝✝✝

ABOUT THE AUTHOR

Paul F.M. Zahl, a retired Episcopal minister,
lives in Florida with his wife Mary. He is the
author of several books, including *Grace in
Practice: A Theology of Everyday Life* (2007),
and is the voice of *PZ's Podcast*.